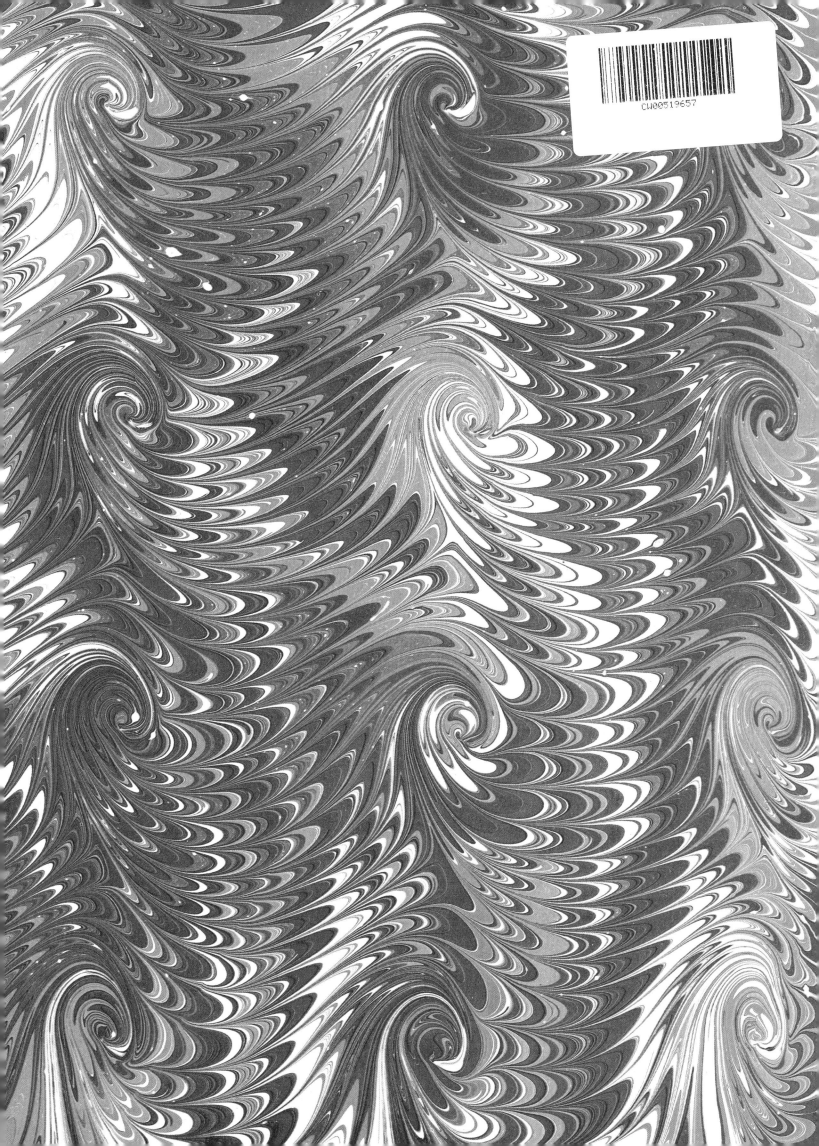

2020

£3.50

14/11

The Perfume Atomizer

An Object with Atmosphere

Tirza True Latimer

Schiffer Publishing Ltd

1469 Morstein Road, West Chester, Pennsylvania 19380

"For Françoise"

Bohemian crystal atomizer with engraved and enamelled decor, c.1934. 4.75" X 3" X 3".

Cover Photo:
"Femme se Parfumant", watercolor and ink, signed "Bénédictus, 1914". Edouard Bénédictus (Paris 1878-1930) was a painter/decorator who began his career in the applied arts as a book binder and later specialized in textile, upholstery and carpet design. Collection: Musée des Arts Décoratifs, Paris. Photo: Laurent Sully-Jaulmes.

Title Page Photo:
Bohemian crystal atomizer; the silver and black enamel decor has wheel-engraved outlines. Mounted and marketed in France in the 1920's. 4" X 4.5" X 1.25". Photo: Parrish Photography.

PHOTOS:

Unless otherwise noted, all objects represented are from the Flamant/Latimer Collection. The heights given are total heights, to the nearest quarter inch, including mount (but not bulb), unless specifically indicated otherwise. The widths and depths are taken at the bases of objects; the height is the first number cited, followed by width and depth, or diameter where indicated. All photographs, unless otherwise noted, are by the author.

Published by Schiffer Publishing, Ltd.
1469 Morstein Road
West Chester, Pennsylvania 19380
Please write for a free catalog.
This book may be purchased from the publisher.
Please include $2.00 postage.
Try your bookstore first.

Contents

Acknowledgments

To those who have so generously contributed the material, energy, advice, expertise, objects, and other forms of support which have made this project pleasurable, as well as possible, I offer my sincere thanks: Cristalleries de BACCARAT; Régine de Robien of BEAUTE DIVINE, 40 r. Saint Sulpice, Paris; Yan Schalburg of BELLE DE JOUR, 7 r. Tardieu, Paris; Maud Bled of GALERIE MAUD BLED, 20 r. Jacob, Paris; BON MARCHE, Paris; Annie Boyer; Patrick Barré of VERRERIES BROSSE, Paris; Véronique Sacuto of CARTIER INTERNATIONAL, Paris; Aracelli Garcia Colombier; Paulette Colombier; Elisabeth Cornu; Sue Cox; Kay and Chris Dann; Sharon Davenport; Linnea Due; Mlle Renaud, Documentaliste, FEDERATION FRANÇAISE DE L'INDUSTRIE DES PRODUITS DE PARFUMERIE, DE BEAUTE, ET DE TOILETTE, Paris; the commendable personnel of the BIBLIOTHEQUE FORNEY, Paris; Patrick Guarisco of MAISON D'ANTOINETTE, INTERNATIONAL, New Orleans; Kurt Preisner of MARCEL FRANCK PARIS; Corbin Gould; Mme Toscany of GUERLAIN, Paris; Laura Israel; Cathy Keyes; Marie Claude Lalique and Danielle Eacher of LALIQUE, Paris; LANVIN, Paris; George and Marian Latimer; Jean Malley; Ellen McGrath; Yvonne Brunhammer, Conservateur en Chef, MUSEE DES ARTS DECORATIFS, Paris; Pascale Bordet and Sonia Edard, Service Photographique, M.A.D.; and, especially, Jean Luc Olivié, Conservateur au Centre du Verre, M.A.D., and Françoise Hugont, Documentaliste, Centre du Verre, M.A.D.; Georges Vindry, Conservateur des Musées de Grasse, MUSEE INTERNATIONAL DE LA PARFUMERIE, Grasse, and Joelle Dejardins of the Grasse museums; Ghislaine Pillivuyt, Conservateur des MUSEES DE LA PARFUMERIE FRAGONARD, Paris and Grasse; Véronique Humbert of the MUSEE DE LA PUBLICITE, Paris; OPTIQUE TETREL, Paris; Evelyne Rochedereux; Claude Bromet and Martine Oswald of the CRISTALLERIES DE SAINT-LOUIS; Nancy and Peter Schiffer; Valentine Schlegel. Thank you to those who choose to remain anonymous.

Finally, my heart-felt thanks to Françoise Flamant for her unfaltering collaboration and encouragement.

Barber's atomizer made of nickel-plated copper with an engraved floral decor, c. 1910. 9'' X 4'' base diam.

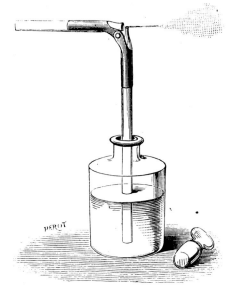

Fig. 71.

Etching illustrating a rudimentary vaporizing technique from *Histoire des Parfums*, Septimus Piesse, 1905. Collection and photo: Bibliothèque Forney, Ville de Paris.

Fig. 72.

Early atomizer illustrated in *Histoire des Parfums*, S. Piesse, 1905. Collection and photo: Bibliothèque Forney, Ville de Paris.

Prologue

The scene was a popular French spa, Pierrefonds; the year was 1859. A certain Dr. Sales-Girons experimented with what he hoped would be an improved treatment for respiratory ailments. He had, to this end, devised a peculiar instrument which "vaporized" mineral waters without altering, as boiling would, their chemical properties. The spa waters, thus vaporized and inhaled, seemed to have a tonic effect superior to that of waters absorbed by the skin or ingested.

The Sales-Girons instrument piqued the curiosity of the medical community. The vaporizing apparatus was presently adopted by Lister to administer disinfectant and antiseptics, and then modified by Richardson to administer local anaesthetics. The Richardson "pulverisor" was the prototype, essentially, for the perfume atomizer.

Until the modern perfume industry emerged, along with the science of synthetic chemistry, in the late 1870's, the atomizer was a primarily masculine device. It was used by the doctor, the dentist, the chemist for the purposes already mentioned, by the farmer and the florist to apply pesticides, and by the barber to condition his gentlemen's beards with perfumed oil.

In 1877, the modern perfume industry was born. Two chemists, a Frenchman, Friedel, and an American, Crafts, together perfected a method of synthesizing aromatic compositions. Here-to-fore, the quantities of raw material required to produce each ingredient of a perfume had been daunting; it took, for instance, 250 lbs. of orange blossoms to extract a single ounce of orange essence. Synthetic chemistry not only dramatically reduced the requirements for raw materials, but

Late 19th century French atomizer. The bottle, despite its lovely fluting and facet-cut collar, retains a slightly pharmaceutical look. 6.50" X 2.50" diam.

PARFUMERIE GELLÉ FRÈRES

EXPOSITION UNIVERSELLE PARIS 1889. MEMBRE DU JURY. HORS CONCOURS

Parfumerie Gellé Frères poster from the Exposition Universelle of 1889. Collection and photo: Bibliothèque Forney, Ville de Paris.

also infinitely increased the possibilities for combining and inventing ingredients while cutting production costs. While retaining its elite image, perfume suddenly became accessible to a whole new class of people. The perfume industry, like everything else that tapped the vigor of the blooming middle class, boomed.

For as long as the domestication of odor has been a preoccupation, so has the diffusion of fragrance. Since the days of the pharaohs, scented substances have been burned, sprinkled, mulled, ground, dabbed, dripped, steamed, fanned, and rubbed into the environment in, seemingly, every conceivable manner. However, at the Paris Exposition Universelle of 1878, the *grands parfumeurs* made a break-through: Guerlain, Molinard, Lubin, among others employed a gadget they referred to as the *"pulverisateur"* or *"vaporisateur"* to entice the passer-by by clouding the atmosphere with their latest creations. Thereafter, the atomizer would become a popular, even essential, feminine toilet article.

Fig. 65. — Bague à jet d'odeur.

The atomizer ring, a novelty pictured in *Histoire des Parfums*, S. Piesse, 1905. Collection and photo: Bibliothèque Forney, Ville de Paris.

Poster for "Parfumerie du Congo", Paris, c.1890, signed "Van Hassel". Collection and photo: Bibliothèque Forney, Ville de Paris.

Poster advertising "Parfums des Femmes de France", signed "Pal", c.1890. Collection and photo: Musée International de La Parfumerie, Grasse.

Early 20th century English atomizer. The polished ebony shell unscrews near its base to receive a replaceable flask of Eau de Cologne. The bottom of the object is stamped "Realyjony". The scent bottle bears the label of "Henry Hodder & Co., Ltd. -Pioneer Cash Chemists—Wine Street—and Branches—Bristol -Bath—and Weston-Super-Mare". 5.50" X 2" base diam.

✤ 9

Advertisement for the "Parfumerie Félix Potin", c.1893. Collection and Photo: Bibliothèque Forney, Ville de Paris.

Bohemian crystal atomizer, c.1900. 7'' X 2'' diam.

The perfume atomizer was soon manufactured and sold throughout the world, though it remains, to this day, an essentially French object, accomplice to fragrance and fashion.

In 1925, *La Parfumerie Française et l'Art dans la Présentation, Revue des Marques,* included the following portrait of the atomizer:

"The atomizer is not a very old invention, but a hearty thing which has quickly eked out a place for itself; is there anywhere in the world in an elegant woman's boudoir where it doesn't occupy the place of honor?

In so far as perfumes have become more subtile and their producers intend a minimum of material to yield a maximum of fragrance, it is more and more necessary to substitute the cloud of perfume for the splash, and that is the function of the atomizer. Thanks to it, the airborne scent insinuates itself everywhere; it lights on the skin, in the hair, penetrates the tufts of the fur coat; and it is the atomizer which permits our modern goddesses to come forth amongst us enveloped in perfumed mists."

Atomizer of Baccarat cut-crystal, flashed with color, c.1895. 6.50" X 2" X 2"

Late 19th century Bohemian crystal atomizer trimmed with gold leaf. 6.50" X 2.50" base diam.

Poster announcing an "Exposition de Coiffures" to benefit the poor...Brussels, 1894. Collection and photo: Musée de la Publicité, Paris.

Two early 20th century English atomizers of cut-crystal with sterling silver pump-mounts decorated in enamel. Left: 5" X 2" diam. Right: 5.50" X 2.50" diam.

Molded crystal travel atomizer with sterling silver pump-mount tooled in a floral motif, c.1900. The inner surface of the mount is entirely gold-plated to protect the integrity of the perfume, as well as that of the metal. A nine-pointed crown, the crown of the counts and countesses, belies the object's noble provenance. Originally, this atomizer must have been a member of a portable toilet set, or *"nécessaire de toilette"*, of many pieces. The silver mount bears two signatures: "P. Jamin", on the inside, and "A.S." with a silver-smith's mark, on the outside. 4.50" X 2.50" diam.

"Parfumerie Rapide William Colsonn" promotes "toilet waters and lotions at reduced prices obtained instantaneously from extracts". The poster, c.1896, is by Misti. Collection and photo: Musée de la Publicité, Paris.

Poster for "Eau de Lubin" by Eugène
Grasset, 1897. Collection and photo:
Musée de la Publicité, Paris.

Chapter One

La Belle Epoque

The turn of the century was the hub of an age of invention. The locomotive, dynamo, telegraph, phonograph, telephone, automobile, and moving pictures were debutantes at the great world's fairs of the late 19th and early 20th centuries. Industrial structures were the new monuments. The Eiffel tower, erected for the Exposition Universelle of 1889, was dressed from head to toe in electric lights for the Fair of 1900 to celebrate *"le siècle de la lumière"*, century of the light, also billed as the "century of Peace, Prosperity, and Progress".

Industry and the People were pictured as advancing hand-in-hand Mammoth new institutions—museums, libraries, department stores— contributed to the popularization of culture and reflected the vitality of the expanding middle class. In this atmosphere of optimism and change, the decorative movement known in France as Art Nouveau literally flowered.

A backlash against what Edmond de Goncourt called the "bric-a-brac-a-mania" of his era, Art Nouveau rejected the hodgepodge of historical references, caricaturizing features of the styles Louis XIV—Louis XVI, which had competed for space in the interiors of the Second Empire. The elements of an Art Nouveau decor were composed by artisans who thought of themselves as *"ensembliers"*; their creations were meant to complement, rather than rival, one another. Art Nouveau, like the Asian Art to which it owed its inspiration, drew its

Fig shaped atomizer decorated in silver overlay. The mount is also sterling silver. American, c.1890. The silver overlay, or silver deposit, technique was particularly well adapted to the flowing lines of the Art Nouveau period. The process, developed in the late 19th century, entailed painting a decor on the glass with flux and then electroplating the object with a metal, which was then hand finished, tooled and/or engraved. 4.50" X 2.25" diam.

lines from nature. Always fluid and organic, the Art Nouveau style imposed a distinct continuity upon its repertoire of motifs. The waterlily, the lizard, the peacock, the bat, the dragonfly, the swan, the iris, the vine, and, above all, the woman, recur, all supple and sinuous, as ornamental themes in every discipline from architecture to embroidery. Taking the female form as an example, she lent herself, body if not soul, to Art Nouveau in the form of various vessels from goblet to vase, pieces of jewelry, or furniture, such as chairs, mirrors, bedsteads, hat-racks; she was the face of a clock, the spout of a teapot; her tresses flowed down the facades of buildings, around lamp-posts, fountains, birdbaths, park benches, the bindings of books and the frames of paintings.

Gallé cameo glass atomizer amidst other Gallé objects. Private collection.

Art Nouveau era atomizer with a realistic salamander motif molded in high relief. The flask is fashioned of nickel-plated glass. The Verreries de St. Denis, and Val St. Lambert, among others, explored the decorative possibilities of metal plated glass early in the century. 9″ X 2.50″ base diam.

By the time the Exposition Universelle of 1900 opened in Paris, the Art Nouveau style was ubiquitous, even oppressive. Known diversely throughout the Occident as Modern Style, The New Art, Liberty Style (England), Stile Liberty (Italy), Jugerdstil, Nieuwe Kunst (Germany), Sezessionstill (Austria), its critics called it "noodle style" and dismissed it as a fad, albeit a long one. By the turn of the century, the English Arts and Crafts movement, which had broken ground for Art Nouveau, was also coming to the end of its road; though Morris & Co. and the Liberty & Co. store were still sound, and the Glasgow Four—Charles Rennie Mackintosh, Margaret Macdonald, and Herbert and Frances MacNair—had a sphere of influence which extended deep into Europe and America as well. In the States, friends of Art Nouveau were still more influential than its foes. Louis Comfort Tiffany, for instance, was at the height of his career. He came home from the 1900 Paris Expo with 3 Grands Prix, 10 Gold Medals, 10 Silver Medals, 2 Bronze Medals, and a Knighthood. The American Arts and Crafts Movement was thriving on the vitality and diversity of designers and artists like Gustave Stickley, Greene & Greene, Candace Wheeler and her Associated Artists, Lucia and Arthur Mathews, and the Roycrofters. In Austria, the late-blooming Viennese Secession was proving worth the wait. Kolo Moser and Joseph Hoffmann were on the verge of creating the Wiener Werkestatte, wellspring of 20th century design.

Two examples of the original Guerlain perfume atomizer, which was produced more or less continuously from the turn of the century until the early 1960's. In the mid-'30s, another model, more modern but of equal simplicity, joined the ranks. Left: 5.25" X 4.50" diam. (Neck of mount signed "Guerlain") Right: 4.25" X 3.50" diam. (Head of mount signed "Guerlain")

Poster for "Lance-Parfum Rodo" by the master of Art Nouveau graphics, Alphonse Mucha, 1898. Collection and photo: Musée de la Publicité, Paris. Copyright © 1992 ARS, N.Y./ADAGP.

Cut-glass travel atomizers with sturdy, leak-proof pump-mounts, c.1910. Left: 4.25" X 1.75 diam. Right: 4" X 1.75 diam. (not including plunger).

Flute-cut crystal travel atomizer, c.1915. The graduated coloring was a popular effect early in the century. 3.50" X 1.25" diam.

Cut crystal travel atomizer flashed with color, c. 1910. 3.50" X 1.25" diam.

Advertisement for Gabilla perfumes,
c.1909.

Men's nickel-plated brass atomizers.
Left: 8.25'' X 2.50'' base diam. Right:
6'' X 2.50'' base diam.

Bohemian, cobalt, cased glass
atomizer, c.1900. 7" X 3.50" diam.

English, brilliant-cut atomizer, c.1910. 4.50" X 1.50" X 1.50"

The flask of this atomizer, c.1913, takes after the era's commercial perfume bottles, which relied more on their labels than their forms for their visual appeal.

Countermovements, of course, were already afoot. In 1901, Matisse, the first Fauve painter exposed his work at the Salon des Indépendants. The *couturier* Paul Poiret announced the *"vêtement libre"*, claiming fashion's first official break away from the full-torso corsets which had constricted women's bodies for generations. He promoted the trend toward bobbed hair or turbans, which eliminated much of the tedium of composing the traditional *coiffure*. The colorful fashion albums created by Paul Iribe and Georges Lepape to advertise Poiret's creations were so innovative that they raised the *métier* of fashion illustration to the level of an art. In 1909, Diaghilev's Ballets Russes opened to sell-out crowds. The sets and costumes designed for the Ballet by Léon Bakst, Matisse, Braque, Sonia Delaunay and others were to have a revolutionary effect on art and fashion. The art scene was rocked by the outbreak of Cubism in 1911.

These events seemed isolated and marginal. But they gave voice to the decorative idioms which would speak for the following decades, if not the century. The *Belle Epoque* and, by and large, Art Nouveau, would not survive the Great War (1914-1918).

Transparent, cobalt glass atomizer, c.1913. The losange shaped spots of enamel coloring the base of the flask create an effect known as Reticello, which originated in Renaissance Venice. The glassmakers of Clichy, north of Paris, specialized in the technique and revived its popularity in the late 19th century. Many dealers loosely describe all manner of colorfully spotted and/or streaked glass as "Clichy".

Signature of Sèvres with interlacing "L"'s, monogram of the monarchs of France. Created in 1738, during the reign of Louis XV, Sèvres has since been, successively, the Royal, the Imperial and the National Manufacturer of Porcelain.

Sèvres porcelain atomizer, c.1915. The celestial blue glaze on the yoke of the bottle is a Sèvres hallmark. 4.50" X 2" diam.

Bohemian cased glass atomizer, c.1913. 4.50" X 2" base diam.

Cartier purse atomizer of white enamel over engraved gold from the 1990 Paris exhibition, "L'Art de Cartier". The ingenious flask-cum-pump design, consisting, basically, of a pair of telescoping cylinders, was reintroduced in the 1920's by Marcel Franck, Aromys, Frégoli, and other manufacturers. Collection and photo: Cartier International.

Purse atomizer created by Cartier in 1912. This example is one of two exposed at the retrospective exhibit, "L'Art de Cartier", in Paris's Petit Palais, 1990. It is fashioned of gold, overlaid with translucent, blue enamel, in the style of Fabergé, and trimmed with a collar of tiny, perfectly matched, half pearls. 3" X 1" diam. Collection and photo: Cartier International.

Léopold and Marcel Franck

La toilette, for the turn of the century woman, was more than a time-consuming daily ritual, it was an institution. Books devoted to the complexities of the toilet and cosmetic arts were best sellers. These books were veritable encyclopedias, offering definitions, indications, cautions and formulas for thousands of beauty potions. This description of Eau de Cologne put forth by the 19th century authority, Arnold J. Cooley, is exemplary: "...a favorite and fashionable scent for personal use and the one most extensively employed. It is also used as a cosmetic, to remove freckles, acne, etc. A very large quantity is likewise consumed by ladies, in high life, as a cordial and stimulant, to drive away vapors and to perfume the breath. For this purpose it is usually diluted and sweetened with sugar, or taken on sugar. A piece of linen dipped in Eau de Cologne and laid across the forehead or on the temples, is a fashionable remedy for nervous headache."

Unusual poster by Misti, c.1895, advertising "Ondine", a rice powder. Collection and photo: Musée de la Publicité, Paris.

These books also contained recommendations concerning the proper furnishing, decoration, ventilation, and illumination of the actual room where these rites were administered; and an extensive list of "articles which should be kept on the table ready for immediate use" was invariably suggested. That this list included the perfume atomizer by the last decade of the 19th century, was largely due to Léopold Franck's willingness to gamble on the future of such an invention.

In 1882, he began to develop the perfume atomizer on an industrial scale—still a new concept. Early on, he established a working rapport with provisioners of quality glassware, such as Baccarat, knowing that his reputation would be built upon the success or failure of his initial models. From his workshop-apartment in a neighborhood of Paris dominated by glassworks, he furnished local hairdressers and beauty product vendors with the first examples of his product. By the end of the decade, Léopold Franck's atomizers were represented in all the fashionable department stores of the city: Le Bon Marché, Le Printemps, Les Galeries Lafayette.

Baccarat and Saint-Louis crystal atomizers by Marcel Franck, c.1915. Collection: Marcel Franck, Paris.

Industrial cameo glass atomizer made for Marcel Franck by Gallé's firm, c.1920. Collection: Marcel Franck, Paris.

Marcel Franck created the mounts
for these atomizers by René Lalique
(left) and Baccarat (right). Collection:
Marcel Franck, Paris.

Enamel glass models created for
Marcel Franck by Gabriel Argy-
Rousseau (left and right) and
Quenvil (center) pictured in Franck's
1924 catalogue. Collection: Belle de
Jour, Montmartre, Paris.

Upon the death of Léopold Franck in 1907, his son Marcel, also an aggressive businessman, took over the direction of the company. As the company expanded, so did Marcel Franck's list of furnishers. He soon had contracts for bottles with the most prestigious glassworks of France, Austria, Germany, Italy, and Bohemia, but he never got so high and mighty as to overlook the talented but obscure local artisan.

Gabriel Argy-Rousseau is a case in point. Later renowned for his work in the difficult medium of *pâte-de-verre*, Argy-Rousseau produced a series of enamelled glass bottles for Marcel Franck early in his career. The simple, clear glass atomizer flasks were decorated with colorful flowers, birds, butterflies, and the like, in a transitional style which leaned more towards Art Deco than Art Nouveau. Most of the bottles were signed or initialed in black enamel. He also executed a few *pâte-de-verre* pieces which bear his signature as well as that of Marcel Franck in molded relief on the bottom of the atomizer. Argy-Rousseau maintained a rapport with Marcel Franck for his bread and butter while his reputation as an artist was building.

While Marcel Franck did occasionally create atomizers for Guerlain, Molinard, d'Orsay, and other *parfumeurs*, as well as furnishing mounts to Baccarat, Saint-Louis, Gallé, Lalique and other glassmakers, his priority was always the promotion of his own mark, the perfection of his own product. Since the production of the flasks was contracted out, the designers employed by Marcel Franck concentrated primarily on the mounts. They developed sophisticated vaporizing systems adapted to a variety of substances (brillantine, perfume, toilet water), or circumstances (the boudoir, the handbag, the steamer trunk),or to harmonize with the style of the object... More about those in the section devoted to mounts at the end of the chapter.

Liter-sized, crystal atomizer with
gilded pomegranate decor, made for
Marcel Franck by Saint-Louis, c.1920.
Collection: Marcel Franck, Paris.

Baccarat

The *flaconnage* produced by Baccarat in the 19th century was, in a word, opulent. Their inventory glittered with flasks of opaline and cased opaline, gem-like cut-crystal doubled and tripled with color, engraved, gilded and enamelled crystal, agate glass and *pâte-de-riz*, all luxury articles of the highest order. Whether inspired by traditional French styles, catering to the vogue for things Gothic, the taste for classical antiquity, or evoking the flavor of Turkey, India, China, the designs were mostly variations on historical patterns, every one of which was ceremoniously conserved in the well defended Baccarat archives.

Baccarat "Eglantier" model; the background of uncolored crystal is acid-etched in a frost-like pattern against which the colored crystal decor stands out in low relief. c.1913. Collection: Beauté Divine, Galerie Régine de Robien, Paris.

Molded crystal atomizer in a gem-cut pattern, colored with enamel, which was produced by both Baccarat and Saint-Louis early in the century. Collection: Beauté Divine, Galerie Régine de Robien, Paris.

Cut crystal atomizer and powder box mounted in ormolu, c.1900.

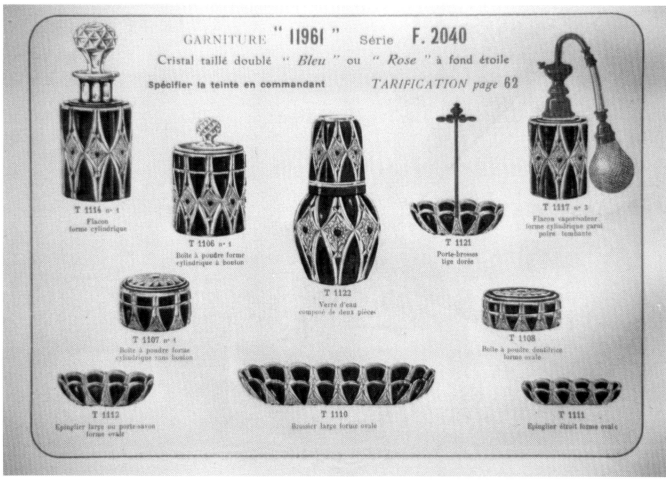

Cased, cut-crystal models from the
1916 Baccarat catalogue.

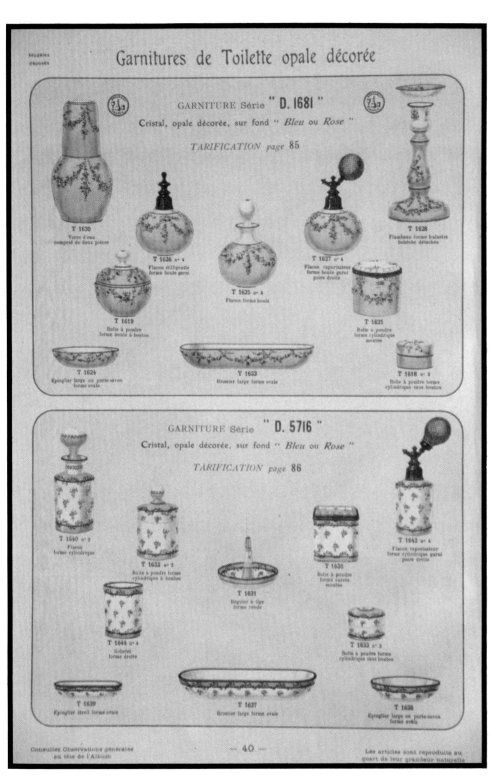

Crystal toilet sets decorated in gilded relief from the 1916 Baccarat catalogue.

Opaline toilet sets decorated in enamel from the Baccarat catalogue entitled *"Garnitures de toilette et articles divers de toilette"* dated 1916.

Enamelled crystal toilet sets, Baccarat catalogue, 1916.

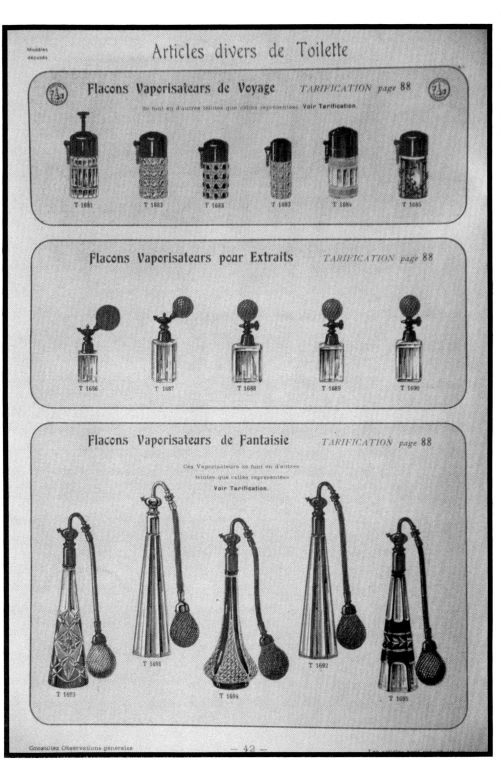

Variety of atomizers pictured in the 1916 Baccarat catalogue.

Generally speaking, a Baccarat atomizer from the pre-war era would have been part of a toilet set, or *garniture de toilette*. A set included as many as 20 pieces. There were flasks of various sizes to contain vinegars for baths and rubs, quinine water and oils for the hair, Eau de Cologne, dental elixir, smelling salts, scents for the handkerchief. There were boxes and jars for almond paste, Vaseline, cucumber pomade, *"poudres de propreté"*, opiate for the teeth and gums; containers for brushes, combs, hat-pins, powder puffs, button hooks, etc. There was a goblet, a carafe, and, of course, an atomizer.

The wheel-cut glass, for which Baccarat is still world famous, was reserved for the most exclusive series. Examples carved in elaborate step-cuts of diamond or star-like patterns were often overlaid with color and sometimes, also, gilt edged, or even dressed in ormolu.

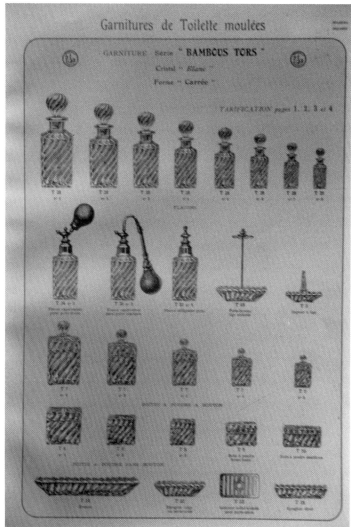

Molded crystal toilet set, Baccarat catalogue, 1916.

Baccarat cut-crystal model in the "Nancy" pattern. Glassware is still produced in this pattern, which was created in 1867. 5.50" X 2" diam.

But even the "Cristallerie of Kings", as Baccarat was known, could no longer afford to ignore the middle class. Relatively inexpensive toilet sets of heavy molded crystal in patterns with names like "Laurier", "Torsade", "Serpentine", and "Russe" accounted for more than their share of the sales. By the turn of the century, these down to earth models could even be purchased from mail-order catalogues and over the perfume counters of departments stores—not the customary Baccarat showplaces.

The Baccarat plant was razed during battle in 1916. Their archives were destroyed, along with everything else. For this reason, as well as for reasons of shifting tastes, only a handful of the turn-of-the-century patterns would be revived after the '14-'18 war.

Baccarat molded crystal model in the "Russe" pattern, c.1916. 6.50" X 2.50" diam.

Baccarat molded crystal atomizers, flasks and *stilligouttes* (sprinkler bottles), began to appear in French commercial catalogues in the first decade of the century. This pattern, called "Torsade" or "Bambous Tors", was the most popular, and has been produced intermittently by Baccarat ever since, with slight variations in the coloration and marked changes in the mount styles. Atomizer pictured, c.1910. 7" X 2.50" diam.

Baccarat molded crystal atomizer in the "Rosaces Multiples" pattern, c.1916. 7.50" X 2.50" diam.

Baccarat molded crystal atomizer, "Serpentine" pattern, c.1916. 6" X 2" diam.

Classic, Saint-Louis satin glass atomizer decorated with a gilded, Empire-style motif of palm leaves in low relief. Collar of the mount is stamped "SAINT-LOUIS". 7.25" X 2.50" diam.

Title page of the 1916 Baccarat catalogue of toilet sets and atomizers.

Unmounted Saint-Louis crystal atomizer bottle, c.1913. The primary layer of uncolored crystal was acid-etched in a fine pattern, creating a satin-like ("*moiré*") effect; the decor, in a relief of colored crystal, was chemically disengaged from the base layer . 6.50" X 2.50" base diam. Collection and photo: Cristalleries de Saint-Louis

Acid-etched, *moiré* glass models decorated in the traditional, gilded motifs identified with Saint-Louis *flaconnage* in the first quarter of the century. Collection: Beauté Divine Galerie Régine de Robien, Paris.

Saint-Louis *moiré* atomizer, c.1920.
Collection: Beauté Divine, Galerie
Régine de Robien, Paris.

Heavy crystal model molded in a
miter-cut pattern, probably Saint-
Louis. c.1915. 7.50″ X 3″ diam.

Archival photo depicting Saint-Louis
atomizers, c.1910 Collection:
Cristalleries de Saint-Louis.

Cover of a 1908 Saint-Louis catalogue bearing the glassworks' trademark. Pieces produced by Saint-Louis were not systematically branded with the logo until late in the 1930's. Prior to that, the use of paper labels was more common. Collection: Cristalleries de Saint-Louis. Photo: Françoise Flamant.

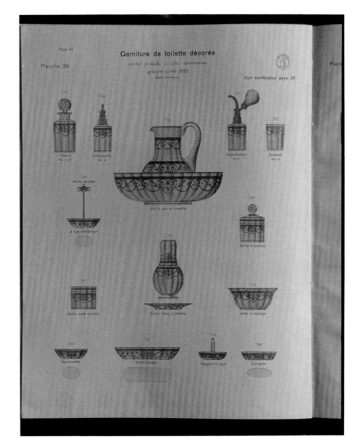

Crystal toilet set in an undulating style known as *"cotes Venitiennes"* with engraved, gilded decor. Saint-Louis catalogue, 1908. Collection: Cristalleries de Saint-Louis.

Cased, cut-crystal toilet sets in the 1908 Saint-Louis catalogue. Collection: Cristalleries de Saint-Louis.

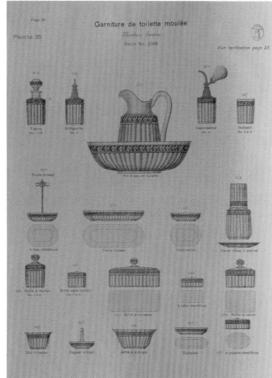

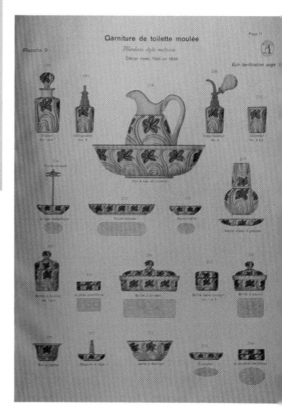

Above and right:
Molded crystal toilet sets from the
1908 Saint-Louis catalogue. Collection: Cristalleries de Saint-Louis.

This Gallé atomizer, c.1920., is a
good example of industrially
produced cameo glass. The morning
glory motif, was first stenciled on to
the vessel, which is composed of two
layers of colored glass. The foreground, violet, was then disengaged
from the background, rose, by means
of a series of acid baths. The decor
was hand finished to sharpen the
details of the resulting relief. 5.5" X
2" base diam.

Gallé and L'Ecole de Nancy

The center of the Art Nouveau movement in France was not Paris, it
was Nancy, capital of the Lorraine, where Emile Gallé, Paul Nicolas,
the Frères Mullers, Schneider, Daum and the others produced works of
art in glass which gave impetus and direction to the decorative
revolution.

L'Ecole de Nancy, founded in 1901 by Gallé, is a phenomenon typical
of that dynamic era: a league of artisans and artists, allied philosophically, forging from their diverse disciplines a common aesthetic. The
development of industrial production techniques would permit the
artists of L'Ecole de Nancy to fulfill what they saw as their destiny as the
"apostles of Color and Line and Beauty".

While Gallé's one-of-a-kind pieces were the basis of his enduring fame
and influence, his firm realized industrially produced cameo glass on a
limited scale as early as 1884. The industrial cameo glass was generally
composed of two colored layers, one for the foreground and one for the
background of the decor, with violet on yellow and red-brown on yellow
being the most common combinations. The quality of these products
was variable in rapport, to a large extent, with the degree of hand
finishing involved in their execution.

"You find in me the proof," Gallé declared, "that neither art nor taste is dependant upon expense." In defense of his involvement with mass production, he claimed, "In my reasonably priced production, I have avoided the false, the grotesque, the frail. My creations have influenced the taste of the larger public. I have prepared the way for production on a grand scale. My work has even been imitated. And it makes me happy!" Indeed, at the time this pronouncement was made, in 1889, some of the most highly regarded glasshouses and artists of Europe could have been considered Gallé's imitators; Saint-Louis, Nicolas, Baccarat, Val St. Lambert, Muller Frères, de Vez, Arsale, Legras, Delatte, Richard, all produced objects advertised as *genre Gallé* or *genre Nancy*.

Gallé's firm was carried on, after his death in 1904, by the momentum of its enormous prestige. It continued to produce art glass until the early '30s. Cameo glass atomizers issued from Gallé's and the other Nancy glasshouses (including those of Daum, Schneider, Paul Nicolas, Muller Frères, and André Delatte) well into the '20s, though the apex of their production was the decade before the First World War.

As the Art Nouveau style lost its hold, as much a casualty of its own success and longevity as of the Great War, many of its initiators foundered. Others, such as Daum, Schneider, and Nicolas, not only survived the post-war reaction against Art Nouveau, but contributed energetically to the creation of the subsequent decorative context, now known as Art Deco.

The Gallé signature, in relief, blends into the decor near the base of the object.

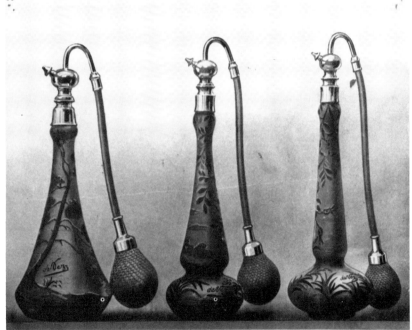

Three cameo glass examples signed "de Vez" from Marcel Franck's 1924 catalogue. De Vez was the pseudonym adopted by Camille Tutré de Varreaux, who became artistic director of the Cristalleries Pantin around 1910. Varreaux designed acid-etched cameo glass products notable for their daring use of iridescent color in one or more of the composite layers; this enhanced the 3-D effect of the often intricate scenes depicted. The iridescent art glass vessels, which include vases, flasks, carafes, and atomizers, are now quite rare. Collection: Belle de Jour, Montmartre, Paris.

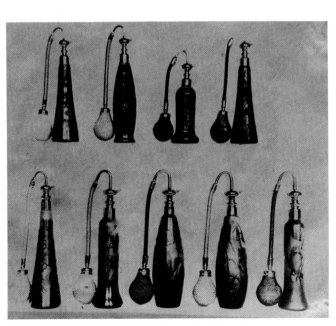

Archival photograph of cameo glass atomizers created for Saint-Louis, c.1910, by Nicolas and Mercier, and signed "d'Argental". Collection: Cristalleries de Saint-Louis.

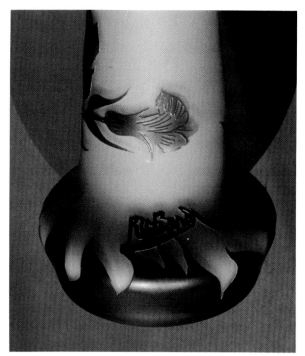

The signature of Richard.

Cameo glass atomizer signed "Richard" in relief near the base, c. 1920. Richard produced 2 and 3 tone, industrial cameo glass in the Art Nouveau style until the late 1920's. Carefully executed in strong, contrasting shapes, and naturalist patterns of considerable delicacy, Richard's products compare favorably to the best industrial Gallé examples of the firm's later period. 7" X 2.50" base diam.

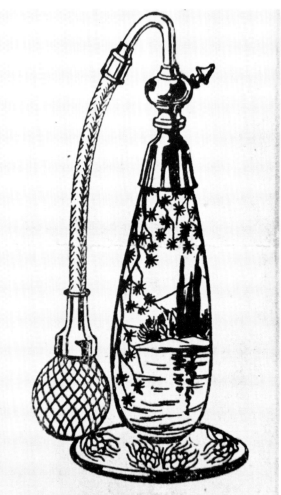

73306. **VAPORISATEUR** cristal d'art "**De Vez**". Hauteur. 0^m,24, monture dorée, balle tombante. . . . . **99** fr.

de Vez atomizer pictured in a 1920 Printemps catalogue.

Daum

Daum of Nancy made its proper mark on the decorative movement set in motion by the founder of l' Ecole de Nancy. While Daum was one of the many glasshouses to produce cameo glass in the style of Emile Gallé, Daum's top-notch artisans and collaborators (many of them, such as Amalric Walter, Jacques Gruber, and Eugène Gall, famous in their own right) carved out a territory for the firm which it dominates to this day. Daum specialized in all manner and combinations of wheel cutting and engraving, acid etching, decoration by incrustation, application, and enamel. Daum excelled in the creation and commercialization of *pâte-de-verre* products. Their mastery of a technique known as *poudres intercalaires*, which rendered a material commonly called jade glass, is especially noteworthy. The translucent, semi-precious stone was simulated by laying powdered enamel colors into the surface of the semi-molten object between layers of clear glass. The technique was used to create a number of effects with color, from subtle graduations to elaborate marbling, as well as to apply more or less precise decorative motifs. Both Schneider and the Frères Muller worked with the colored powders, too, but only Daum worked magic with them.

Daum atomizers are very rare and precious to collectors, often showing off a surprising combination of the qualities for which the signature is revered.

This rare atomizer, c.1910, represents a combination of techniques characteristic of Daum. The "jade glass" flask was acid-etched for a satin finish and then embellished with a fuchsia motif in fired-on enamel. The "Daum Nancy" signature, in low relief near the object's base, is punctuated, as was their custom, with the doubled cross of Lorraine. 5"x 2.5".

DeVilbiss perfumizer, c.1925.

De Vilbiss

In America, the DeVilbiss "perfumizer" was the queen of them all. The company's founder, Dr. Allen DeVilbiss, was a nose and throat specialist. He developed a medicated oil which could be sprayed into the throat, a less painful and more sanitary treatment for infections than the common practice of applying the remedy with a cotton swab. Dr. DeVilbiss patented the atomizer he devised for this use and, in the late 1880's, established the DeVilbiss Company to manufacture the atomizers. Dr. Devilbiss' son Thomas became a full partner in the company in 1905 and, despite several years worth of objections on his father's part, he eventually launched what he hoped would be a lucrative sideline of atomizers modified for perfume.

The first DeVilbiss "perfumizers", as they called them, were actually crystal salt-cellars fitted with atomizer mounts. Almost immediately, the perfumizers outsold the medical atomizers so that a vindicated Thomas DeVilbiss was able to devote most of his energy to developing the aspect of the business he had championed.

Thomas DeVilbiss designed the majority of the company's early perfumizers, from its first, in 1909, through the late 20's. His mount designs, unusual enough to warrant patenting, were elaborately decorative: One of the most extraordinary took the form of a stylized vine with the flask suspended from its tendrils like a piece of exotic fruit; another resembled a dragonfly in flight.

Eccentric mount designs became, in fact, the unofficial hallmark of DeVilbiss products. In the '30s, Frederick Vuillemenot designed crystal atomizers with mount-heads which were crested by elaborate tiaras of bohemian cut glass, as if to disguise the mount as a stopper. Vuillemenot and fellow designer Carl Sundberg up-dated the DeVilbiss image for the '40s, introducing steamlined mounts and bottles whose forms were contoured to one another. The '50s, the "New Look" era, brought outrageous, neo-baroque mounts which sprouted bouquets of cultured pearls on gilded wire stems. Even the most run-of-the-mill DeVilbiss mounts were distinctive, "graceful tops", as a catalogue from the '20s proclaimed, "posed like the buds of rare flowers"; they are as good as a signature for purposes of identification, though most DeVilbiss products were signed.

Thomas DeVilbiss, like his French counterpart, Marcel Franck, combed the U.S. and Europe to secure contracts with glassworks for the fabrication of flasks for his perfumizers. His network of suppliers circled the globe, including the Steuben, Imperial, Cambridge, and Vineland Flint Glassworks in the U.S., Daum and Brosse of France, Moser of Bohemia, and various other companies in Czechoslovakia, Germany, Italy, and Japan. Some of the bottles, such as those manufactured by Steuben, Imperial, or Daum, were finished products, needing only to be mounted as atomizers upon arrival at DeVilbiss, while others were so-called blanks, to be decorated on site at the DeVilbiss plant.

The DeVilbiss catalogues, fanciful masterpieces of commercial art themselves, catered to the full spectrum of tastes. Hundreds of options were displayed, from the gaudy, verging on grotesque, to the simply elegant. Aglow, as one catalogue put it, with "a wealth of rainbow radiance", many of the brightly colored atomizer bottles were high-lighted with gold leaf, gilded metal applique, or gold incrustation, which aimed, according to the same catalogue, to "introduce a pleasantly ostentatious note" to the collection.

The DeVilbiss company was among the first to exploit the market for iridescent glassware which developed early in the century. A wealth of archaeological treasures was then being unearthed in the near and middle east. Intriguing glass artifacts, like the pieces which had inspired

Louis Comfort Tiffany, were making the rounds of the major museums. The characteristic iridescence of this ancient Greek and Hebraic glass resulted from centuries of exposure to the earth's corrosive salts. The ingenious Tiffany had been able to counterfeit the effect by spraying his near molten glass forms with a mist of acids in which, it is said, he had dissolved $20 dollar gold pieces to add luster to the iridescence.

Frederick Carder, one of the founders of Steuben Glass, devised a technique for mass producing Tiffany-style lustre glass under the trade name, Aurene. Between 1902 and 1930, Steuben turned out thousands of Aurene perfume bottles and atomizers, in both lustrous gold and peacock blue, many of them for resale under other marks, such as DeVilbiss.

The graceful Aurene glass models, created for DeVilbiss by Steuben, vied for popularity with the all time top-selling Imperial Jewel Glass series, manufactured by the Imperial Glass Co. for DeVilbiss in their patented emerald-, ruby-, pearl-, or amethyst-colored iridescent glass during roughly the same period.

The first third of the century was the heyday of the DeVilbiss perfumizer. The company continued to manufacture atomizers until 1969, when perhaps they suspected that the "Renaissance of Femininity"—heralded by their own 1930s ad campaign—was over.

T. J. Holmes

The T.J. Holmes Co. of Massachusetts has been producing atomizers for longer than any other company in America. The company's founder, Thomas Jefferson Holmes, patented his first perfume atomizer in 1876, though the medical atomizer was the company's original and most important product.

Early Holmes perfume atomizers bore the trademark "Favorite". Later generations were brand-named "Holmespray". Like DeVilbiss and Marcel Franck, T.J. Holmes Co. did not manufacture their own bottles; though, judging from the number of patents accorded to company officers and employees, they took an active interest in bottle design. They also designed and manufactured the mounts for their atomizers.

Mounts

The mount of a perfume atomizer is an important feature for several reasons. Most obviously, the mount is that which defines the object, which differentiates the atomizer from the flask, which gives the atomizer its distinct appearance, its separate history. Because the mount invites the handling of the object, it is also what gives the atomizer its peculiarly intimate nature. Rose Nicolle, in her World War One era beauty primer, *Une Idée de Parisienne par page*, colorfully described the object's magnetism: "...And if there is an atomizer, you surrender at once to the desire to possess a little of its perfumed star-dust; your hand nervously, as in an avid caress, grasps and squeezes the little rubber bulb."

For the collector, the mount may help to authenticate or date a piece, though all too frequently the original mounts have been replaced. A substitution involving a new mount is easily detected, as is the use of an older mount from a different period than that of the bottle. If the original mount has been replaced by a mount of the appropriate style, a sharp eye can still often spot the switch. If the collar attached to the neck of the bottle is made of a different material than that of the screw-on head of the mount, the head is from another bottle. The head, for instance, may be lead with a gold finish, and the collar gold-plated brass. A close look at existing knicks or scratches will reveal the discrepancy in the

This late 19th century *"pisseur de parfum"*, fashioned of bisque porcelain, has numerous female counterparts in collections such as those of the Musée International de la Parfumerie, Grasse, France, and the Musée de la Parfumerie Fragonard, Paris and Grasse. French experts attribute the pissers' origins to Germany, whereas German authorities cite France as the provenance. Collection: Musée de la Parfumerie Fragonard, Paris.

colors of the base metals. Sometimes, too, the threads inside the collar may prove to be of a slightly different caliber than those of the head, while still permitting a fit. The collars are cemented to the flasks with a thin layer of plaster which would normally become discolored as the perfume permeated it over the years; if the mounting plaster looks too clean, it may mean that the original collar has been soaked or cut off the bottle and that the whole mount, collar and head, has been replaced. (Or it may just mean that the atomizer was not used much.)

An atomizer which retains its original mount, even a damaged or dysfunctional mount, is worth more to the collector than an atomizer which has had an alien mount grafted on to it. A dealer, though, will sometimes boast that an atomizer has been newly mounted and is in perfect working order, thanks to his or her considerable trouble and expense. A well restored atomizer is, of course, more valuable and more interesting than a poorly restored or incomplete atomizer, providing the buyer knows the difference.

The earliest perfume atomizers were typically fitted with mounts which functioned by means of one or two rubber bulbs hung from a length of tubing which joined the head of the mount at a right angle to the flask. Pumping the bulb created enough pressure within the flask to force the perfume up a glass pipette into the head of the mount and hurl it against the pin-hole opening at the end of a long, beak-like nozzle. The beaked format, later equipped with a single bulb screwed directly into the head of the mount, without the intervening tube, was the norm for decades, eventually disappearing in the early 1920s.

This turn of the century flute-cut atomizer is equipped with its original mount, though the rubber tubing and bulb have long since disintegrated. 6.50" X 2" diam.

Bouquet of pre-World War II atomizer bulbs.

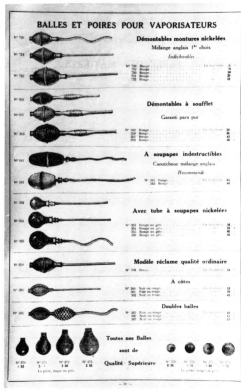

Page from an early Kitzinger Frères catalogue illustrating the various atomizer bulb options. Collection: Belle de Jour, Montmartre, Paris.

Opposite page:
Late 19th century Bohemian crystal atomizer with pump-mount (left) and cased glass atomizer with "swan's neck" mount (right). Collection and photo: Marcel Franck, Paris.

Classic flute-cut atomizer, c.1900, with beaked mount and original rubber bulb. The mount's collar is stamped ''B.C. Brevet [patent] S.G.D.G.''. The bowl at the top of the collar is designed to catch any drips running down the nozzle and redirect them back into the bottle. 7'' X 2.75'' diam.

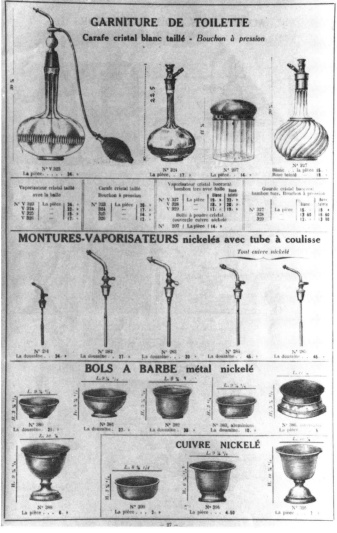

Page from Kitzinger Frères catalogue advertising a selection of adjustable, replacement mounts. Collection: Belle de Jour, Montmartre, Paris.

Various piston pump systems also were common before and after the turn of the century. These were less perishable, but expensive to produce.

The graceful "swan's neck" mount, an aptly Art Nouveau conception, was quite popular in the gay '90s. In 1901, the translation of *A Thousand and One Arabian Nights* became a best seller in France and a mount resembling Aladin's lamp came on the scene. In 1927, Charles Lindbergh's landing was wildly celebrated in Paris. Around that time, an aerodynamic mount style was introduced; this rocket-like mount perched on its bottle as if ready for take off. It became the mount most typical of the '20s.

The crown-like, piston pump mounts made for Lalique and others by Marcel Franck in the '20s were as artful as their flasks. Their success undoubtedly proved to other manufacturers that the mount could and should be considered a major factor in the overall decorative impact of the object.

Flute-cut travel atomizers like these, with their compact pump-mounts, were fabricated from the turn of the century until the 1940's. The plunger pushes down into the mount head and locks in with a quarter turn clockwise. A screw-on cap, insurance against leaks, is chained to the nozzle. 4" X 1.50" diam.

Heavy, molded crystal model in Baccarat's "Diamants Pierreries" pattern, c.1916. The Aladin's lamp mount was in fashion for the first two decades of the century.

Glass atomizer with World War I era mount style. 4" X 2.50" diam.

Molded glass atomizer of a pattern offered by Kitzinger Frères in their 1929 catalogue. The aerodynamic mount style is characteristic of the 1920's. 5.5" X 2.50" base diam.

Travel atomizer with the basic "Le Parisien" mount by Marcel Franck, c.1924. "Le Parisien" and "Le Provençal" are essentially the same model; the degree of tooled, molded, or engraved decoration varies.

Group of "tango" colored, double crystal atomizers, c.1926. The profile of the swan's neck mount became increasingly less bulbous as the decade progressed.

Most early mounts were fashioned of pewter, tin, or molded lead, usually finished in nickel or gold plate or leaf. The piston pump mounts were an exception; these were built, at least in part, of more durable metals like brass, bronze or silver.

By the mid-1920s, Marcel Franck, for one, had come to the conclusion that brass was the most suitable material for a mount. Thereafter, all Marcel Franck mounts were made of chrome-plated or gold-plated brass. Most Marcel Franck mounts were named, ... "Fizz", "Super-Fizz", "Le Parisien", "Le Provençal", "L'Escale"..., and patented. By 1930, brass mounts were standard pretty much everywhere.

In the '30s, mount styles were nearly as various as bottle styles. The mount, chrome-plated and geometric to suit modernist tastes, had become the decorative summit of the atomizer, much as the stopper would be to a flask. Thereafter, mount styles more or less followed atomizer styles which continued to follow decorative trends, for better or worse.

"L'Apothéose", another mount by Marcel Franck, was created in 1950 for the perfume of Christian Dior. The lacy design picks up on the super-femininity of Dior's "New Look".

Double crystal atomizer with colorful, fired-on enamel decor. Collar of the mount is stamped "Fizz Made in France". Fizz is the name of this mount style, introduced by Marcel Franck in 1928. The Fizz prototype made its debut atop the centerpiece of the Marcel Franck atomizer display at the Exposition des Arts Décoratifs of 1925: a Baccarat tour-de-force of cased, cut crystal which stood nearly two feet tall and took 6 months of continuous work to realize.

Marcel Franck mounts. Left: "Super Fizz" (1935), Center and Right: "L'Escale" (1936). These systems are entirely metallic, eliminating perishable rubber parts. "L'Escale" (which translates "port of call") is a travel atomizer; the disk-shaped metal pump rotates over the head of the mount opening or closing a gate valve within. Guaranteed not to leak, "L'Escale" is perhaps the most sophisticated mount ever made; it is composed of 26 solid brass parts, each of which was electroplated three times to assure the durability of the finish.

Molded glass atomizer made in France, c.1948, with a screw-on, aluminum pump replacing the traditional rubber bulb. 3.50'' X 3.50'' diam.

Crystal atomizer, c.1930, with chrome-plated, pentagonal mount. 6.50'' X 2.50'' base diam.

Prismatic, cut crystal atomizer with typical 1930's mount style. 4'' X 2'' X 2''.

Chapter Two

The Art Deco Era

The discerning Frenchwoman of the 1920's led an art-rich life. From the largest element of interior decor, perhaps a lacquer screen signed "Jean Dunand", to the most intimate detail, a hairbrush created by Paul Iribe, she composed her environment of objects born of a generation of artists whose mission it was to bring art to life... to everyday life.

The works of Sonia Delaunay were hung in the wardrobe more often than in the gallery. "If art has entered everyday life," she declared, "it is because women carry it on their backs." Delaunay and other avant-garde artists, like Nadezhda Udaltsova and Alexandra Exter, designed clothing, handbags, china, tablecloths, umbrellas, as well as costumes and sets for theater. Sophie Taeuber-Arp laid the groundwork for the De Stijl movement, applying complex theories of form and color to everyday objects, furniture, stained glass, and especially textiles. Gunta Stölzl, technical head of the Bauhaus weaving workshop, and her protegées, Otti Berger, Benita Otte, Anni Albers, and Margarete Leischner, followed in Taeuber-Arp's footsteps. Marianne Brandt, a graduate of the Weimer Art Academy, was the author of a wide variety of industrial

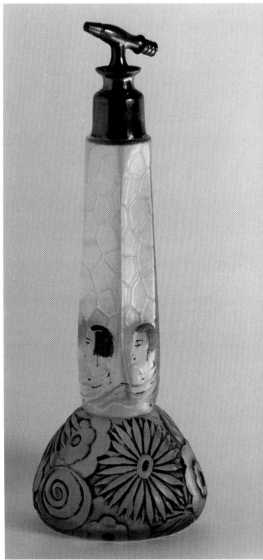

Frosted glass atomizer, c.1925. The molded profiles encircling the neck of the bottle are touched up with paint and a violet stain highlights the Art Deco bouquet which embellishes the base. 7" X 3" base diam.

Photograph of a storefront from a 1925, Paris, Exposition des Arts Décoratifs catalogue entitled *Façades et Agencements de Magasins.* Collection and photo: Bibliothèque Forney, Ville de Paris.

Enamelled glass atomizer, c.1922, with a charming, orientalist decor; signed "V. de France." 6" X 2" base diam.

Frosted glass atomizer, c.1925. A rust colored stain sets off the molded relief of the geometric decor. 6.50" X 2" X 2".

designs, including cooking utensils, wall-brackets, teapots, shaving mirrors, and adjustable bedside and desktop lamps. Paul Iribe's delicate fancy touched the powder box, the hand mirror, the candlestick. Marie Laurencin was routinely called upon to collaborate with the fashionable decorator, André Groult. Laurencin designed frames for her paintings, and created paintings for the interiors for which she had created the wallpaper. She, too, designed sets for the theater. Slade School trained painter turned decorator, Eileen Gray, fabricated the frames for a number of paintings in the personal collection of Jacques Doucet. This launched her on a twenty year adventure with the Oriental art of Lacquer. Gray's screens, tables, chairs, light fixtures and decorative panels were often exposed in conjunction with the rugs and wall hangings of another interior artist, her old friend Evelyn Wyld. The resulting environments were striking to the point of being controversial. Raoul Dufy manufactured masterpieces in wallpaper as well as in fabric and upholstery. René Lalique, forsaking jewels for glass, signed his name to bookends, picture frames, lamps, clock cases, hood ornaments, vases, carafes, and flasks. Even Cartier had taken a practical turn, introducing banalities such as letter openers, compacts, and pillboxes and pocket-atomizers to his exclusive collection of jewelry.

French atomizer, c.1925, the glass is finished with a semitransparent, iridescent lacquer over a painted decor. 7.50'' X 2'' base diam.

Porcelain model with cherry decor, c.1925, signed "Limoges France". The collar of the mount is stamped "RLB". 5'' X 1.5'' base diam.

Molded glass atomizer, c.1920. The original price tag on the bottom of the flask indicates that Henri Hutte of Meudon was the vendor and that the price was 13F25, about the same as the price of a pair of silk stockings, at the time. 7.50'' X 2.50'' diam.

♣ 53

Opaque glass atomizer decorated in paint with the Art Deco rose. 6.50" X 2" base diam.

Frosted, molded glass atomizer, c.1925. 5" X 2" base diam.

Frosted glass model with enamelled decor, c.1925. 6" X 2.5" base diam.

1925, the year of the first major world exposition devoted entirely to the decorative and industrial arts, was the high-point of the era of exaltation for the every-day object. The revolutionary technological advances which stole the show at the Universal Exposition of 1900, had become standard industrial procedure. An *objet d'art* which would have been produced as a unique piece or in a limited series in 1900, was mass produced in 1925.

The perfume atomizer, indispensable feminine accessory, was typical of the humble objects transformed by the verve of the Art Deco designers into veritable masterpieces. For today's collectors of Art Deco objects, glass, or perfume bottles, atomizers of the inter-war era constitute an under-exploited, and often under-valued, repository of quality period pieces. Paul Poiret's Atelier Martine, Charles Schneider, Marcel Goupy, Robj, Viard, DeVilbiss, Georges Chevalier, Sabino, and, above all, René Lalique designed Art Deco perfume atomizers which have become museum pieces.

Travel atomizer of opaline cased crystal, c.1922. Mount stamped "Made in France." Original vendor's sticker on bottom reads, "Parfumerie—Maroquinerie—L. Crouau—49 rue Lévis". The price was 28 francs.

French atomizer, c.1925. of glass painted with an iridescent, opaque lacquer. 5.50" X 1.25" X 1.25".

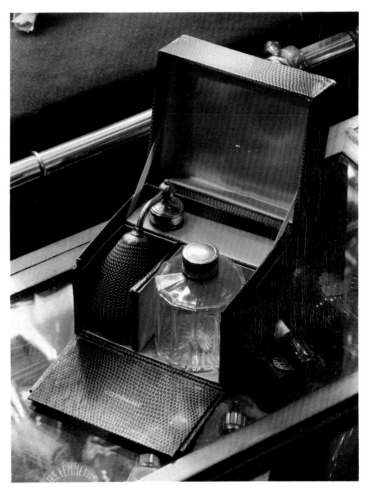

Crystal flask/atomizer with customized box, elegant packaging for Coty's 1927 perfume, "L'Aimant". Collection: Belle de Jour, Montmartre, Paris.

Photo-Rep. — Hélio, Faucheur, Chelles   *Ch. Moreau, éditeur, 8, rue de Piague - Paris (XIIᵉ)*
· PARFUMERIE ·.
Raguenet et Maillard, architectes.
Sculpture de Binet. — Verreries de Lalique.

"Figurines Drapées Dansant" travel atomizer originally created by René Lalique in 1924 for Marcas et Bardel, of molded, patinated glass. Signed "R.Lalique Made in France". 3" X 1.25" diam. Photo: Parrish Photography. Copyright © 1992 ARS, NY/SPADEM.

A fountain of glass created by René Lalique as the centerpiece for the Pavillon de la Parfumerie at the Paris Expo '25. Collection: Musée des Arts Décoratifs. Photo: L. Sully-Jaulmes. Copyright © 1992 ARS, NY/SPADEM.

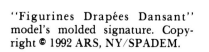

"Figurines Drapées Dansant" model's molded signature. Copyright © 1992 ARS, NY/SPADEM.

René Lalique

Just as the 1900 Paris Exposition had been a milestone in René Lalique's career as an Art Nouveau Jeweler, so was the 1925 Expo an affirmation of his triumph as a glassmaker and his vision as a designer.

From the time, in 1907, when François Coty commissioned the young Lalique to design labels for his perfume and got back bottles instead, to the time of Lalique's death in 1945, René Lalique designed hundreds of bottles, all of them treasures, for the perfumes of Coty, Worth, d'Orsay, Roger & Gallet, Molinard, Lubin, Lucien Lelong, and scores of classic flasks, atomizers, and toilet sets for his own Lalique & Cie.

Realized in the sophisticated, molded glass he popularized, many of René Lalique's atomizers from the '20s and '30s were designed with such enduring appeal that two generations later they are still produced by Lalique. The models "Duncan", named for Isadora, and "Dahlia" are exemplary. Atomizers produced during René Lalique's lifetime, though, are easily distinguished from more recent editions; for one thing, they are signed "R. Lalique", "R. Lalique France", or "R. Lalique Made in France". The initial "R" was dropped from the signature soon after René Lalique's death in 1945. Otherwise, mount-styles help to identify a model's era, as does the nature of the material; contemporary Lalique creations and re-creations are realized exclusively in crystal.

Perfume atomizer created for Worth's "Dans la Nuit" by René Lalique in 1924. A firmament of stars, molded in low relief, studs the globe-shaped flask which is imbued with a deep blue patina. Collection: Belle de Jour, Montmartre, Paris. Copyright © 1992 ARS, NY/SPADEM.

Today's "Garniture de Toilette Duncan", signed "Lalique France", is fashioned of crystal. The "Duncan" motif was created by René Lalique in 1931. The original model, a travel atomizer with pump-mount, was realized in molded, partially patinated glass. Collection and photo: Lalique, Paris.

"No.2 Dahlia" atomizer, 1931, of uncolored, molded glass with a satin finish. Signed "R.Lalique France" on bottom of flask. 7" X 5" max width X 2.50" max depth. Copyright © 1992 ARS, NY/SPADEM.

The "Cactus" travel atomizer, created by René Lalique in 1943, was originally realized in molded glass with a satin finish. The current Lalique "Cactus" toilet set is of satin-finished crystal, pointed in enamel. Collection and photo: Lalique, Paris.

Contemporary Lalique crystal "Garniture de Toilette Dahlia." Collection and photo: Lalique, Paris.

A few of Lalique's atomizer designs from the early '20s, such as "Epines" and "Papillons," are reminiscent of his Art Nouveau jewelry motifs. Most of his decors, though, whether floral ("Mimosa", "Fleurettes", "Marguerites") or composed of his characteristic figurines, are definitively Art Deco. The figurine motif has a number of different manifestations: haunting "Sirènes", cherubic "Enfants", exotic "Danseuses Egyptiennes", statuesque "Duncan". A motif advertised by Molinard as "Bacchantes", of which there were several variations, graced many of Lalique's travel atomizers. Girlishly insouciant nudes sporting flowering garlands, romping voluptuaries, or sedately draped ladies striking classical poses, René Lalique's figurines encircled, in precise relief, a flask sized to fit a woman's hand. The flask was crowned with a gilded pump-mount often decorated, itself, to complement. Lalique designed a number of these travel atomizers for perfume companies such as Molinard and Lubin. Usually commissioned to promote a debutante scent, the Lalique travel atomizers were the direct forebears of the dispensers in which nearly every eau-de-toilette is available today.

Robj, Sabino, Viard, Geneviève Granger and Lucille Sévin of Etling, Hunebelle, and scores of other memorable and less memorable decorative artists produced Lalique-style *flaconnage* in the '20s and '30s, but no one approached the standard set and maintained by René Lalique.

"No. 4 Epines", a molded glass model with blue patina, was created in 1920 by René Lalique and signed "R. Lalique France" on the bottom of the flask. Lalique preferred to work in glass, more malleable, though less prestigious, than crystal; his chosen metal proved irreproachably responsive to the intricacies of the molds he created. 6.50" X 3" diam. (Part of this example's mount if missing.) Copyright © 1992 ARS, NY/SPADEM.

1949 Molinard catalogue picturing Marc Lalique's re-edition of the "Octagonal Quatre Figurines" travel atomizer originally created by René Lalique for Marcas et Bardel in 1927. The mount, in both cases, was made by Marcel Franck. Collection and photo: Bibliothèque Forney, Ville de Paris.

François Coty, one of the first to capitalize upon the notion that the package is as important as its contents, chose a young jeweler, René Lalique, as his collaborator in 1906. The choice proved pivotal to the history of glass as well as to that of modern marketing. Lalique, having abandoned gems in favor of glass, went on to design and manufacture countless commercial perfume bottles during his long career; he set the standard for the many who would follow in his footsteps, including his son, Marc Lalique, who succeeded him as the head of the firm, and his granddaughter, Marie Claude Lalique, the company's current guiding light. This atomizer, a model called "Figurines et Guirlands", c.1924, is one of several made for the perfume company Molinard. The model was advertised by Molinard as "Bacchantes". The mount, "Le Provençal", is by Marcel Franck. The flask is fashioned of molded glass finished in a soft, sea-green patina. The embossed signature on the bottom of the flask reads: "R. Lalique Made in France". 4" X 1.25" diam. Copyright © 1992 ARS, NY/SPADEM.

Charles Schneider and Le Verre Francais

Originally employed by Daum, Charles Schneider was one of the first artists of the Nancy School to cross the frontier between Art Nouveau and Art Deco. The distinctive Schneider style, which used Art Nouveau techniques to express Art Deco motifs, caught on and, in 1918, Le Verre Français was founded in order to mass produce Art Deco cameo glass. Le Verre Français, under the direction of Charles' sister, Ernestine Schneider, fabricated cameo glass atomizers between 1918 and 1930. These were aggressively colored in two or three contrasting hues; azure, tango orange, violet, lemon, coral, indigo, and umber were favorites. The decor, whether orchid, belladonna, panther, scarab, or lizard, was always exuberant, exotic, and highly stylized. Most of these cameo glass atomizers were signed "Le Verre Français", though a few, singled out for production a more limited series, were signed "Charder", a contraction of Charles Schneider. The Charder examples are considered the most outstanding.

Cameo glass model produced by Charles Schneider's company, Le Verre Français, c.1920. The signature is hand engraved in script on the bottom of the flask. 6.50" X 4.25 diam.

Baccarat crystal atomizers decorated in enamelled patterns created by Georges Chevalier. Marcel Franck catalogue, 1924. Collection: Belle de Jour, Montmartre, Paris.

Georges Chevalier at Baccarat

Georges Chevalier, like most of the great Art Deco designers, was the master of a number of disciplines. Architect, sculptor, painter, and foremost designer/decorator for Baccarat, Chevalier's most historically acclaimed accomplishment was the creation of the dazzling Baccarat-Christofle Pavilion at the Paris Exposition of 1925. The glassware he designed for that event would completely over-haul the tradition-bound Baccarat image. To Chevalier, crystal was not so much the medium for the decor as the decor itself, a concept which still seems fresh today. The *flaconnage* produced during Chevalier's tenure was exceptional, even for Baccarat. Atomizer versions of the classic bottles created for Gabilla, Lubin, Guerlain, and other *parfumeurs*, were a big success with their clientele; and Baccarat had a hard time keeping up with demands for the toilet sets Chevalier designed. His work celebrated the purity of the material; like water or ice, Chevalier's crystal seemed to both capture and radiate light. The fluid "Draperie" series of flasks and matching atomizer which he created for the 1925 Exposition is the quintessence of the Chevalier style.

Chevalier is less well known than many of his equals (and, indeed, his inferiors) as his pieces, according to the tradition at Baccarat, do not bare his signature, but solely the signature of the house. A certain amount of documentation permitting the positive identification of his creations has been published, however.

Heavy, molded crystal atomizer from a set originally designed by Georges Chevalier for the Baccarat display at the Paris Expo '25. 6" X 4" max width X 3" max depth.

Gabilla perfume catalogue, 1930, picturing bottle with matching atomizer (bottom) by Baccarat. Mount by Marcel Franck. Collection and photo: Bibliothèque Forney, Ville de Paris.

Atomizer signed ''MF'' (Marcel Franck) and ''Baccarat'', c.1925. The quintessential Art Deco decor is lightly acid-etched on the surface of the characteristically pure Baccarat crystal.

Baccarat crystal atomizer and matching flasks designed in 1925 by Georges Chevalier. The molded scallops of the decor are outlined in gold. (Atomizer mount not original.) Collection: Maud Bled Galerie, Paris.

Group of Marcel Franck atomizers, c.1925. Collection: Marcel Franck, Paris.

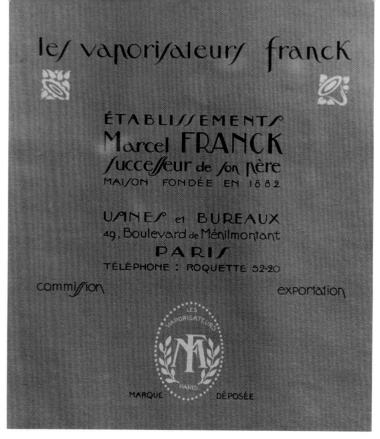

Title page of Marcel Franck's 1924 atomizer catalogue. The trademark at the bottom of the page was frequently used to sign Art Deco era Marcel Franck products. Collection: Belle de Jour, Montmartre, Paris.

Cover plate for the chapter entitled "Mes Porcelaines d'Art" of Marcel Franck's 1924 catalogue. Collection: Belle de Jour, Montmartre, Paris.

Cover plate for chapter entitled "Mes Cristaux Taillés" of the 1924 catalogue which illustrated models of classic cut and/or acid-etched crystal executed for Marcel Franck by Baccarat and Saint-Louis. Collection: Belle de Jour, Montmartre, Paris.

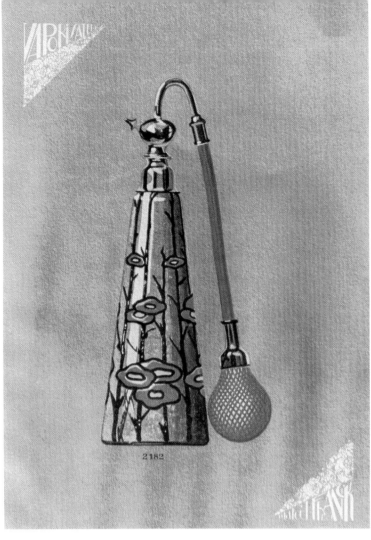

Marcel Franck atomizer of glass decorated with gold incrustation, c.1925. Collection: Marcel Franck, Paris.

Cover plate for chapter entitled "Mes Emaux Translucides" of the 1924 Marcel Franck catalogue. Collection: Belle de Jour, Montmartre, Paris.

Amber colored, cut crystal atomizer, c.1928, by Marcel Franck. 7.50" X 2.50" base diam.

Marcel Franck, double crystal atomizer decorated in gold leaf and gold incrustation, c.1925. Collection: Marcel Franck, Paris.

Viard

The Verreries Viard of Montreuil, a Parisian suburb, was widely recognized in the 1910's and 20's for its delightful molded glass perfume bottles, flasks, and atomizers.

The gay, Art Deco bottles, signed "J.Viard" in molded relief, were designed primarily by Julien-Henri Viard, a sculptor turned glass merchant, whose partners in the business were C.Viard, R.Mouquet, and G. Violet le Duc. The Societé des Artistes Français' catalogue for the Salon of 1906 describes J. Viard as the student of C. Viard and A. Mercié; Antonin Mercié was a monumental sculptor of the Beaux Arts tradition.

The relationship between the C. & J. Viard glassworks of Montreuil and that of Gabriel and Eugène Viard of Bar-sur-Seine is unclear, perhaps non-existent, though the two are sometimes confused. (The Bar-sur-Seine glassworks is remembered as the site where the great Maurice Marinot, Fauve glass-artist, mastered his craft.)

J.Viard perfume atomizers are still relatively affordable, and absolutely charming, Art Deco ornaments.

Cover of Verreries Viard publicity brochure, c.1925. Collection and photo: Cristalleries de Saint-Louis.

Glass model signed in the mold, "J. Viard France", c.1925. A red stain offsets the decor, figuring birds and flowering vines.

Example signed "J. Viard Made in France" in relief on bottom of flask. The molded leaf and berry decor is accented in enamel and backed up by a light stain. Fabrication of the blanks for Viard's bottles was probably subcontracted out, but it is likely that the decorative finishing touches were done on the premises.

Photograph from the "Poiret le Magnifique" exhibition catalogue (Paris, 1974) picturing a collection of outsized perfume bottles and atomizer decorated by l'Atelier Martine in the 1920's. Collection and photo: Bibliothèque Forney, Ville de Paris.

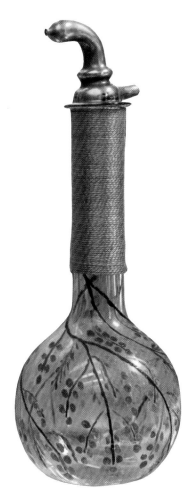

Poiret's "Nez"/chemist, Shaller (inspired, perhaps, by the glassware which equipped his perfume laboratory) suggested the form of this Rosine atomizer. The blanks for the model were executed in Murano and then decorated by hand by the Martines. Collection: Musée de la Parfumerie Fragonard, Paris.

Paul Poiret and the Martines

In 1911, Haute Couture's prodigy Paul Poiret became the first fashion designer to market his own line of perfumes. He called his brand Rosine, for his first born daughter. Once François Coty had overcome his initial disdain for the couturier's venture into an unfamiliar domain, he made several futile attempts to buy out Poiret's instantly successful business. With Rosine, Poiret promoted the lingering notion that "a woman's scent is her unique signature". Gabrielle Chanel later followed suit with her "No.5" and the ensuing trend had a lasting effect on both the fashion and the perfume industries, linking them irrevocably.

Simultaneous to founding Rosine, Poiret opened a school of decorative arts for talented girls without means or prospects; He named the school Martine, for his second daughter. The students, girls of 12 and 13, were eager and gifted, though "unspoiled" by formal training. Poiret took them on sketching expeditions to the zoo, the Jardin des Plantes, up the Seine to the country. He took them to Sèvres to observe the decoration of porcelain, to the atelier of Raoul Dufy to watch him print. The Martines were taught to weave, to decorate ceramics and glass, to print wallpaper and fabrics, to paint murals. They were introduced to Matisse, Van Dongen, Rouault, and other painters. And then they were set loose to create.

Poiret was so taken with their creations that he soon established a decorating business, also called Martine, where the older girls were employed. Their boldly colored fabrics and wallpapers, in patterns with names like "Cyclamen", "Artichauts", "Begonias", were all the rage, as were their *haute-laine* rugs. They painted murals in theaters, restaurants, offices, shops, and homes—Isadora Duncan's home, for one. They also designed many of the products and packages for Rosine.

Exotic scents smelling, according to one Rosine catalogue, "like the light mist of the morning" or "evoking the atmosphere of the beloved bedroom of which one dreams", and boasting names like "Fruit Defendu", "Minaret", and "Borgia", were presented in dramatic containers which are highly prized by collectors today. The bottle for the scent called "Le Balcon" featured a miniature balcony fashioned of real cast iron around its girth; "Mouchoir" was nestled in a silk handkerchief.

The Rosine atomizers, hand-painted in one-of-a-kind motifs representing under-water scenes, bees swarming on the flowering mimosas, dragonflies, and ferns, to name a few, were as original as any of their creations. Fashioned after the designs of Poiret's perfume chemist, Shaller, by Murano glassmakers, these blown glass atomizers in exotic and attenuated forms were exceptionally fragile. Even the mounts were made of blown glass. Few have survived intact to this day, though a number of splendid examples are preserved in the collections of the Musée International de la Parfumerie in Grasse and the Musée de la Parfumerie Fragonard, Grasse and Paris.

Blown glass atomizer with dragonfly decor hand painted by the Atelier Martine for Paul Poiret's perfume company, Rosine. Collection: Musée de la Parfumerie Fragonard, Grasse.

1922 Rosine catalogue featuring blown glass atomizers, hand painted by Paul Poiret's Atelier Martine. Collection and photo: Bibliothèque Forney, Ville de Paris.

Interior of the river-barge/houseboat "Amour", one of three such *peniches* decorated by the Atelier Martine for Paul Poiret's exhibit at the Paris Expo '25. Several Martine perfume bottles and an atomizer ornament the lavatory table top on the left.

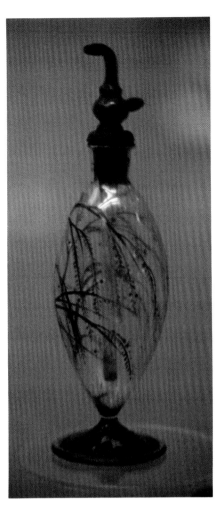

Rosine blown glass atomizers hand painted by the Martines. Collection: Musée International de la Parfumerie, Grasse.

"Le Kid" decorated in enamel. 2.50" X .75" diam.

"Le Kid" finished in mother-of-pearl, checkerboard inlay. 2.50" X .75" diam.

Brass and nickel-plated brass "Le Kid" pocket atomizers, c.1925. 2.50" X .75" diam.

Though the name Poiret is mainly associated with the years leading up to the First World War, his exuberant innovations, and those of the Martines, exerted an undeniable influence on decoration right up to the financial crash of '29. His house, like so many others, foundered then and exuberance was no longer the order of the day.

Five years after the release of Chaplin's celebrated film, Marcel Franck introduced an atomizer of the same name, "Le Kid". A more modest version of the deluxe pocket model created by Cartier in 1912, "Le Kid" was the darling of the Marcel Franck display at the Paris Expo '25. "Should not a woman, at any moment, in any place, be permitted to create a lingering, perfumed wake?" posed Marcel Franck in *La Parfumerie Française et l'Art dans la Présentation, Revue des Marques, 1925.* Franck gambled that the answer would be "Yes" and invested massively in the production of "Le Kid". Available in a multitude of finishes, including nickel or gold plate, mother-of-pearl, enamel, shagreen, tortoise shell, galalith, lizard, eel and snake skin, "Le Kid" was as big a hit for Marcel Franck as it was for Chaplin. Collection: Marcel Franck, Paris.

In 1925, Cassandre, Grand Prix de l'Affiche, launched the publicity campaign for "Le Kid". Copyright © 1992 ARS, N.Y./ADAGP.

This example was made by Marcel Franck for d'Orsay, c.1926. "Le Kid" is engraved on the inner cylinder, "Parfums d'Orsay Paris" on the bottom of the outer shell. 2.50" X .75" diam.

Brosse

The Verreries Brosse has been in existence since 1854. Originally not a glass producer, but a contractor in utility glass, Brosse took on a new dimension in 1919 when the ownership was assumed by Emile Barré. Barré bought up and consolidated several small glass factories which had previously been his subcontractors and proceeded to develop the design, production, and retailing aspects of the business under the same umbrella. Brosse teamed up with St.Gobain in the mid-20's to create a fully automated bottle producing facility, a strategy which proved pivotal for both companies in the struggle to survive the world economic crisis and the Second World War.

Emblem designed for Jeanne Lanvin by Paul Iribe representing the elegant Madame Lanvin embracing her daughter, Marie Blanche.

Created in 1927, Lanvin's classic "Boule Noire" was the result of a collaboration between Armand Rateau (bottle design) and Paul Iribe (emblem design). Madame Lanvin's home was furnished with other stylish creations by Armand Rateau; her Rateau boudoir has been reconstructed by the Musée des Arts Décoratifs, Paris, and is permanently displayed there. The "Boule Noire", produced through the years in various dimensions with a variety of stoppers or mounts, was, and still is, fabricated by the Verreries Brosse. Collection: Verreries Brosse, Paris.

1984 Lanvin advertisement introducing a contemporary version of the "Boule Noire" atomizer (Verreries Brosse).

‡ 71

Atomizer bottle design by G. Schwander for Kitzinger Frères, c.1925. Schwander had his own business until the mid-1930's when he was absorbed by the Verreries Brosse, where he continued as their primary designer for decades. Collection: Verreries Brosse, Paris.

Members of the third Barré generation are the current directors of Brosse, whose headquarters are still in Paris, and, now, in New York as well. Though still an important retailer of standard pharmaceutical glass, the factories proper to Brosse, fully computerized, now produce exclusively perfume bottles. Some familiar examples include: Nina Rici's "L'Air du Temps" with its Lalique-designed stopper, Jean Patou's "Joy", "Opium" by St.Laurent, "La Nuit" by Paco Rabane, Carvan's "Ma Griffe", as well as lines of image-making flasks linked with the names Chanel, Guerlain, Lanvin, Hermes, Fabergé, not to mention the flask-art of Paloma Picasso.

Brosse has fabricated generations of blanks for the atomizers of companies such as DeVilbiss, Kitzinger Frères, Marcel Franck, and Step, as well as product-associated atomizers for Lanvin, Guerlain, Hermes and many other perfume houses. Brosse bottles are sometimes marked "VB", or "BR" followed by a model number, but are often not signed.

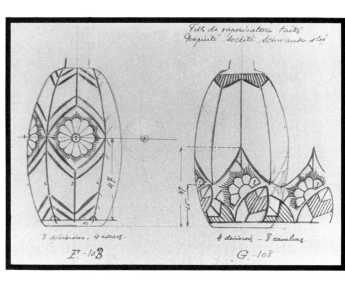

Two schematic drawings for cut-glass atomizer flasks by G. Schwander, c.1922. Collection: Verreries Brosse, Paris.

Design for atomizer, c.1925, by G. Schwander. Collection: Verreries Brosse, Paris.

Robj

In other times, one said of a woman:

'...such a pretty thing.' And that meant: '...a curio, pleasing to look at, but, well, at best, to be put on a shelf from which to be knocked, one fine day, by a blow from a feather duster...' It is no longer permitted today to speak this way of a woman, nor of a curio. One, like the other, is indispensable. If you don't know that, you are a frightful reactionary, and you have never set foot chez Robj.

Noel Pibrac, 1927

The quote above is extracted from an article which appeared in *La Demeure Française*, and was inspired by the Robj display at the Salon d'Automne of 1927. This is one of many articles devoted to the collections presented in the 1920's by the ceramics and glass editor Robj, a pseudonym derived from the decorative artist's actual name, Jean Born. In 1926, a reviewer for *Mobilier et Décoration* described Robj as: "The creator of the modern curio..." who "...awakens the sense of humor..." with his "...ironic Parisian spirit." In their catalogue of atomizers, Briau advertised *"modèles inédits de* Robj" along side those of Gallé, Saint-Louis, and Baccarat. René Lalique collaborated with Robj to create a series of part ceramic, part glass, electric perfume burners which apparently glowed while perfuming the atmosphere. In 1929, a critic writing for *L'Amour de L'Art* predicted that "...in a hundred years, one will collect the knick-knacks of Robj as one now collects the 'Queen Victorias' and 'Prince Alberts' which issue from the kilns of Staffordshire."

Collectors today do collect Robj, yet the name figures only as a footnote in the back pages of most contemporary reference books on the decorative and ceramic arts of the 1920's.

Molded glass atomizer with a decor of tropical birds and vegetation, signed "Robj Paris" in the mold. c.1927.

L'ENVOL

LAMPE DE BUREAU
CÉRAMIQUE D'ART

BIBELOTS
D'ART

Robj

5 cité d'Hauteville

PARIS

1929 ad for the Robj boutique from the *Magazine Renaissance de l'Art Français et des Industries de Luxe.*

Robj was a sculptor who had found his niche designing and producing small, more or less useful, objects, mostly in ceramics. In his studio, near the heart of Paris's ceramics and glass district, he displayed the amusing personality decanters ... the friar, waiter, baker, gendarme, judge, choirboy... and the novelty bookends, perfume burners, soap dishes, candlesticks, and inkwells for which he became, briefly, famous.

In his day, Robj employed many would-be sculptors, encouraging them to explore the possibilities offered by a career in the applied arts. He sponsored an annual contest to promote excellence in the field of industrial design, offering cash prizes to the winners in addition to contracts for the production of the winning designs.

The nature of the objects Robj proposed for execution in glass, judging by the atomizers, seems to have been less farcical than his ceramic fantasies, though they are still light-hearted. The atomizers are a component, however minor, of what another contemporary reviewer referred to as Robj's "daily contribution to what will remain of our 20th century".

On the heels of "Le Kid," Aromys of Paris announced its latest product: "l'Aiglon" (the eaglette) "for the purse, the pocket, the voyage." "L'Aiglon", originally offered in three sizes and at least eighty styles, gives "Le Kid" a run for its money. This example, finished in mother-of-pearl panels with an engraved and gilded, floral decor, was one of the twenty mother-of-pearl models featured in Aromys' 1929 catalogue, which presented matching compacts, lipsticks, and cold cream boxes, as well..."the prettiest gifts to offer, the best received." 2.25" X .50" diam.

Robj atomizers were signed "Robj Paris" in the mold; this example also retains its original paper sticker indicating model number, decor, and price.

Frosted glass atomizer, c.1927, with the Robj signature incorporated in its molded decor. "Le Secret de Robj", a perfume, and Robj-brand perfumed pastilles were advertised as accessories to his atomizers and perfume burners. 5" X 2" base diam.

Cover of Aromys's 1929 catalogue for their pocket-sized atomizer, "l'Aiglon". Collection: Belle de Jour, Montmartre, Paris.

Nacrolaque model (similar to Bakelite). 2.50" X .75" diam.

"Aiglon" with floral motif executed in galalith, an early plastic product. 2.75" X .75" diam.

Deluxe model in mother-of-pearl. 3" X .75" diam.

Galalith "Aiglon" figuring a stylish, young woman hopping into the passenger's seat of a sports car, an example of what the catalogue described as "the most beautiful decorations in Parisian taste". 2.75" X .75" diam.

Bohemia: The Land of Glass

While the impact of the designer-celebrity on his or her culture and environment cannot be denied, it is often the cumulative effect of anonymous objects which creates the texture of a decorative era. Art Deco atomizers in forms and finishes from the sublime to the ridiculous were mass produced in the '20s and sold by the hundreds of thousands over the perfume counters at Le Printemps, Galeries Lafayette, Le Bon Marché, Harrod's, Wanamaker's, Bloomingdale's... Estimating conservatively, half of the models on the world market in that decade issued from Bohemia, including the area known as Czechoslovakia in modern times.

Glass in the images of polished onyx, veined malachite, marble and jade, iridescent luster glass, fluorescent "uranium glass", brilliant ruby and cobalt cased-glass, glass cut like gem stones in topaz, amethyst, sapphire, and amber: These are among the innovative shades and effects which secured Bohemia's identity as an industrial entity, however difficult it was to define her territorial frontiers prior to 1918. The world's most important exporter of glass since the late 17th century, Bohemia was renowned for the business acumen, as well as the skill, of her glassmakers.

This sarcophagus-shaped double crystal atomizer, c.1925, testifies to the era's appetite for antiquity which was whetted by the excavation of Tutankhamon's tomb in 1922.

Six piece double crystal toilet set, c.1925. Bohemian double crystal, a variety of cased glass, was a fad of the jazz era. Double crystal atomizers were produced in a variety of lively colors (ruby red, jade green, ultramarine blue, "tango" orange, coral, lemon yellow...) and fanciful shapes (spinning top, amphora, bell...). The outer layer of glass was uncolored, magnifying the intensity of the opaquely colored, inner layer. Atomizer 4.50" X 3" diam.

Marbled double crystal
toilet set, c.1925. Atomizer
6'' X 2'' base diam.

Bohemian double crystal atomizer,
c.1925. 4.50'' X 2'' base diam.

Bohemian double crystal atomizer
shaped like a spinning top, c.1925.
3.50'' X 3.50'' diam.

Bohemian double crystal atomizer
with original bulb, tube, and netting,
c.1925. 6.50'' X 2'' base diam.

The dappling at the base of this
double crystal atomizer, an effect
described as *"moucheté"* (which
translates "fly-specked"), is worthy
of a more elegant name. c.1925. 6.50''
X 2.50'' base diam. (Mount not
original.)

As a rule, Bohemian glass agents worked together for the purposes of exportation, which permitted them, collectively, to flood the world markets with relatively high quality products at relatively low prices. The majority of the utilitarian glassware in France, for example, early in the century, was Bohemian.

Bohemian glass was rarely signed by the manufacturer or artist. The provenance of even the most distinguished pieces was often indicated, if at all, in the most general terms, usually marked simply "made in Czecho-slovakia", though occasionally a signature would include the name of the contractor, such as I. Rice, Ingrid, or "M.F." for Marcel Franck.

Bohemian glassworks were represented by agencies in hundreds of European and overseas cities. These agencies, in place since the 18th century, were the nerve ends of the industry. Each Bohemian apprentice was required to spend a minimum of two years in the service of an agency in order to qualify as journeyman. This practice assured the industry a steady flow of information and inspiration from abroad.

Bell-shaped double crystal atomizer with green and white streaking, c.1925. 4" X 2" base diam.

Group of double crystal atomizers, c.1925.

Double crystal atomizer with matching powder box, c.1925. Atomizer 6.50'' X 2'' base diam.

Bell-shaped Bohemian double crystal atomizer, c.1925. 7'' X 2.50'' base diam.

Streaked ("*tigré*") double crystal atomizer, c.1922. 7" X 2.25" base diam.

Double crystal atomizer decorated with a cased-in confetti of enamel. Bulb and tube original. c.1925. 7.50" X 2.50" base diam.

The Bohemian glass industry, as a result, had its ear to the ground in 1929 and responded quickly to the turn-about in fashions precipitated by the world economic crisis. The bright and bombastic double crystal atomizers which had captured *les années folles* were phased out. The new forms were strictly angular, fashioned of transparent crystal in subdued colors, or sculpted of massive uncolored crystal and starkly decorated in enamel, usually black enamel.

Czechoslovakia continued its unparalleled exportation of all manner of glass products until the partition resulting from the conference at Yalta frayed, if not severed, her ties with the West in 1945.

Double crystal atomizer with black crystal base and original bulb and tube, against a backdrop of a matching perfume burner (left) and powder box (right). Private collection.

Bohemian double crystal atomizer in tear drop shape, with gilded metal base, c.1925. Collar of mount is marked "RLB". 7.50" X 2" base diam.

Pieces from a double crystal *garniture de toilette* which probably originally included additional flasks, with stoppers, and a powder box.

Double crystal atomizer, Bohemian c.1926. 5'' X 2'' base diam.

Bohemian double crystal atomizer, c.1925. 6.50'' X 2'' base diam.

Amphora-shaped, Bohemian double crystal atomizer, c.1925. 6.50'' X 2'' base diam.

The End of an Era

Art Deco is the loose term under which we now regroup the objects produced in the 1920's. The title was contracted from the Exposition Internationale des Arts Décoratifs et Industriels, the name of the Paris Expo of 1925. The Expo '25 was the high point of this overall decorative context, and the point from which it naturally began to decline. The era, known as the "age of optimism", "the roaring 20s", "*les années folles*", with its diversity of artistic influences, its passion for ornamentation, its taste for the exotic, the outrageous, was not destined to fade gracefully away. It ended abruptly on Thursday, the 24th of October, 1929, when the New York Stock Exchange was forced to close its doors against the stampede of panicked investors which had over-run Wall Street. When those doors opened again, they opened upon a sobered world.

Crystal atomizer with geometric decor in acid-etched relief, c.1929. 6" X 2.25" X 2.25".

1920's style, cased glass atomizer. Collection: Beauté Divine, Galerie Régine de Robien, Paris.

Ceramic pocket atomizer signed "Paradis France". The name refers to the rue de Paradis, heart of Paris' glass and ceramics district. This example was fabricated by Kitzinger Frères, 15 rue de Paradis, Paris, c.1925. 3.25" X .75" diam.

Houbigant's facet-cut atomizer created for "Essence Rare", c.1929. (Mount not original.) Collection: Galerie Maud Bled, Paris.

✤ 85

Compartmentalized travel atomizer; each of the four nozzles corresponds to a distinct chamber within the flask. c.1924. Collection: Musée International de la parfumerie, Grasse.

This ceramic Buddha with sleeping beauty in his lap is one of the exceptional perfume atomizers displayed at Paris' Bon Marché in the context of their unprecedented exhibit "Le Parfum et ses Merveilles" (1991). The piece, c.1927, is signed "Royal Dux," of Bohemia. Collection: Belle de Jour, Montmartre, Paris.

Man's nickel-plated pocket atomizer, c.1920. 2" diam. X .50" depth.

Dual-purpose purse atomizer, c.1925, signed "Frégoli". The outer cylinder contained perfume, the inner cylinder (which is also the plunger for the atomizer) contained a tube of lipstick. Frégoli was the name of one of the era's most popular comedians, a renowned quick-change artist.

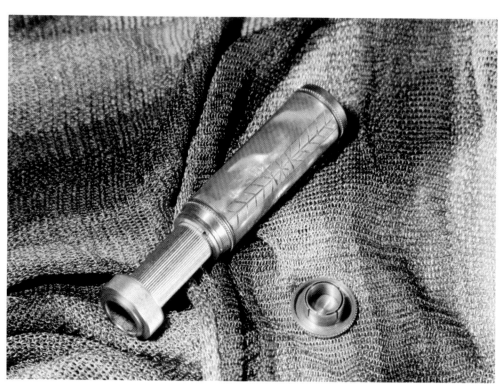

Moiré crystal atomizer decorated in a gilded, Louis XIV-style motif, created for Mignon by Saint-Louis c.1928, signed "Mignon" on bottom of flask. 4.50" X 1.50" base diam.

Flute-cut, conical atomizer of graduated , violet-colored crystal, trimmed in gold. Saint-Louis, c.1922. 4.50" X 1.50" base diam.

Flute-cut crystal atomizer with graduated coloring. Probably Bohemian. c.1925. 4.50" X 3" diam.

Conical, flute-cut crystal atomizer, c.1930. *Flaconnage* of this style was generated in quantity by the glasshouses of Bohemia as well as by certain French firms, such as Saint-Louis. 8'' X 2'' base diam.

This example dates from the late 1920's; the classic, flute-cut, conical form and graduated coloring were very common from around the turn of the century until well into the 1930's; the mount styles changed more or less by the decade.

Cylindrical, flute-cut crystal atomizer, c.1923, of a style manufactured in Bohemia or in France during the first three decades of the century. 6'' X 2.25'' diam.

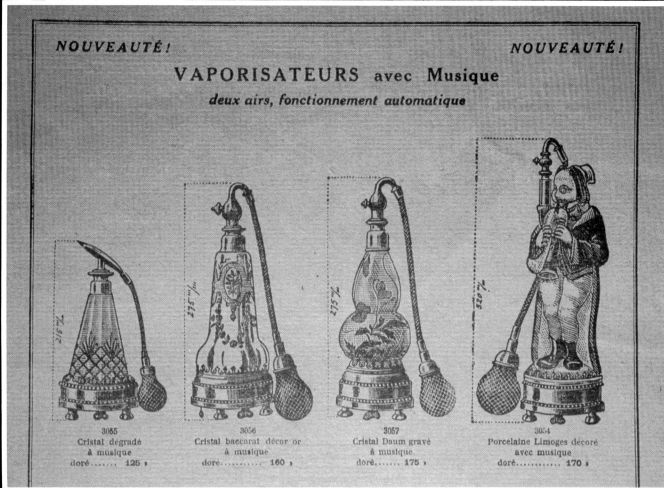

VAPORISATEURS avec Musique
deux airs, fonctionnement automatique

3055	3056	3057	3054
Cristal dégradé à musique doré...... 125 »	Cristal baccarat décor or à musique doré.......... 160 »	Cristal Daum gravé à musique doré...... 175 »	Porcelaine Limoges décoré avec musique doré............ 170 »

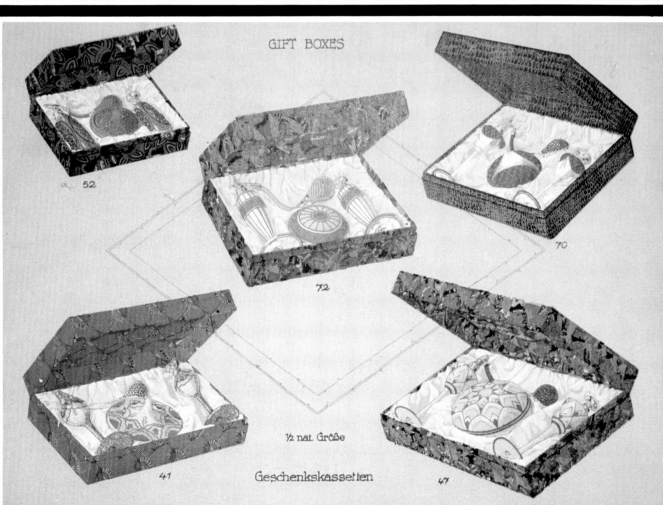

GIFT BOXES

52

70

72

41   ½ nat. Größe   47

Geschenkskassetten

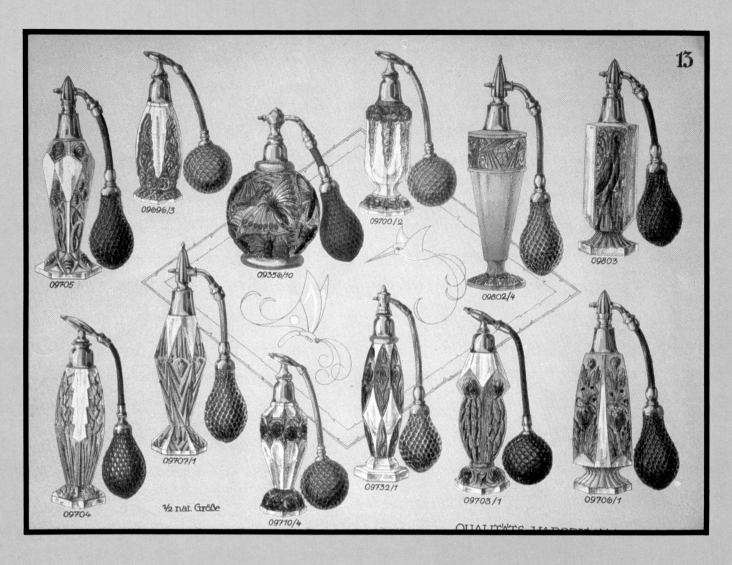

09696/3

09356/10

09700/2

09802/4

09803

09705

09707/1

09704

½ nat. Größe

09710/4

09732/1

09703/1

09706/1

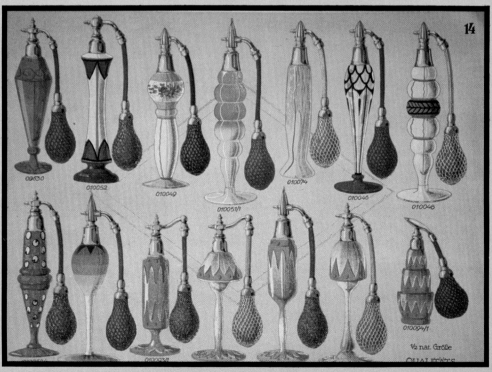

09630

010052

010049

010051/1

010074

010046

010048

010094/1

½ nat. Größe

Pages figuring perfum atomizers from a German catalogue of unknown origin dated 1929. Private Collection. Photo: Jacques Meyer.

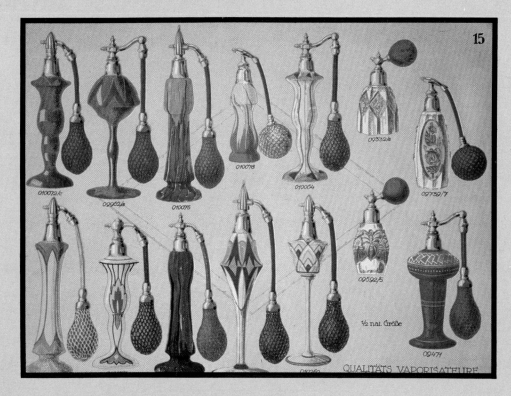

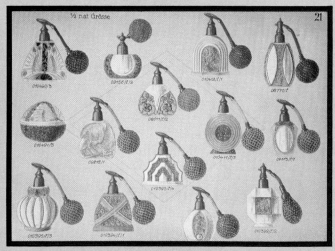

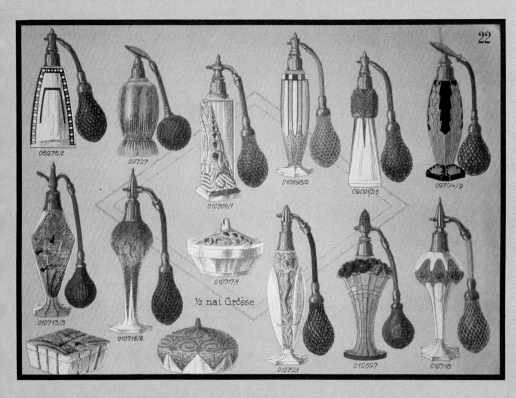

Bohemian crystal atomizer with black and silver decor, c.1930. 4" X 4.50" X 1.25".

Bohemian crystal atomizer with engraved and enamelled decor. c.1934. 3.75' X 2.50" X 2"

Bohemian enamelled crystal atomizer , c.1930. 5" X 2.50" X 1.75".

Chapter Three

"*Design or Decline*"

The world economic crisis accelerated the final phase of the 1925 style. Even at the style's apex, critics had reproached certain high-rolling Art Deco designers for their insensitivity to the needs of the larger society and the problems imposed by modern life. Within the design community of the '20s, these concerns were voiced by what seemed, at the time, to be a puritanical faction, a kill-joy fringe of technocrats devoted to Functionalism, Modernism, Cubism, or Bauhaus architecture. These Modernists were to become design's key players between the crash of '29 and the onset of the Second World War.

Marcel Franck's "Fizz", c.1930, with Bohemian enamelled crystal flask. 3.50" X 1.25" X 1.25".

Bohemian crystal atomizer with engraved, enamelled, and frosted decor in a geometric motif which picks up on the form of the bottle. The mount is signed "Vapolux", a trademark used by Kitzinger Frères in the 1930s. 4.25" X 4" X 2".

Another version of Marcel Franck's "Fizz", c. 1930. The flask, with etched, frosted, and enamelled decor, is of Bohemian crystal. 4" X 3.50" X 3.50".

"Fizz" atomizer by Marcel Franck, c.1930. The Bohemian crystal flask is decorated in enamel. A black glass medallion bears the initial "M". 3.50" X 2.50" X 1.50".

"Super-Fizz" by Marcel Franck, c.1935. The decor of the flask is engraved, enamelled, and, in places, frosted. "Tchecoslovaqie" is hand etched on the foot of the flask. 3.75" X 4" X 2"

Black glass atomizer trimmed in gold with perfume burner of a similar style, c.1930. The atomizer is unsigned. The perfume burner is signed "Catalyseur ERELBE" and "RLB Made in France". Atomizer 4.25" X 2.25" X 2.25".

The Modernist style was characterized by an efficiency of line, a reliance upon form for its esthetic impact, a reverence for geometry, a subtlety of texture, and a structural simplicity which aimed to facilitate both the production and the up-keep of the product. Modernism's elements were industrial more than organic: chrome, steel, patent leather, and glass. Its colors were sober: black, silver, grey, beige, pale rose, mint green, and ice blue.

Modernist rhetoric unanimously condemned the employment of "useless" ornamentation... though an ornament in the shape of a triangle did seem to qualify, somehow, as less useless than an ornament in the form of a rose. More than one critic was irritated by the double standard; Léon Werth, reviewing the 17th Salon des Artistes Décorateurs for *Art et Décoration* (1927), dismissed Cubist-style decoration as "caprice disguised as geometry".

Whatever the ins-and-outs of fashion, one thing was certain given the economic climate: fine artists, artisans, decorative artists, and manufacturers needed to put aside their rivalry and reconcile themselves to a unprecedented degree of cooperation for the sake of their mutual survival. In the commercial and industrial sectors, the in-house artist, once a luxury, had become a necessity. The artist-directors and art staffs of the design centers affiliated with Paris's biggest department stores (La Maitrise of the Galeries Lafayette, Pomone of the Bon Marché, Studium of the Louvre, and Primavera of Le Printemps) were undoubtedly to be thanked for the solvency of their umbrella institutions during the leanest years.

Crystal atomizer, c.1934. The collar of the mount is stamped with the name of the German cosmetics company "Scherk". 5.50" X 5.50" base diam.

Crystal atomizers; flasks signed "Tchecoslovaquie"; mount of rear model signed "Sélection Made in France".

Bohemian cut-crystal example, c.1937. 4" X 5" X 2.50".

Bohemian glass products from the 1930's often bore an acid-etched or engraved mark identifying their provenance. Alternatively or additionally, there may have been a paper label like this one which read, "Cristal de Bohême". The origin of this glass was considered a strong selling point and such labels were usually prominently displayed. 3.50" X 3.50" diam.

Bohemian cut-crystal atomizers, c.1930. Variations on the model were produced by the hundreds of thousands in the early 1930's. The sharp line, subtle colors and transparency of the material represent the gist of the about-face in fashions precipitated by the world economic crisis. 4" X 4.50" diam. (rear), 3.50" X 4" diam. (front)

Bohemian flashed crystal atomizer with gilded decor which could be described as what one contemporary design critic called "caprice disguised as geometry". c.1931. 4.50" X 5" max width X 2.50" max depth.

Advertisement from *Renaissance de l'Art Français et des Industries de Luxe*, 1929, for Maurice Dufrène's gallery, La Maitrise, with-in the Parisian department store Galeries Lafayette.

Bohemian crystal model, c.1937. Collar of mount stamped "Czechoslovakia"; mount originally chrome-plated. 3" X 3.25" X 2.25".

Bohemian crystal atomizer, c.1935.
4.50'' X 2'' base diam.

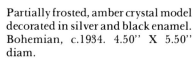

Bohemian crystal atomizer, c.1930.
3'' X 3'' X 3''.

Partially frosted, amber crystal model
decorated in silver and black enamel.
Bohemian, c.1934. 4.50'' X 5.50''
diam.

Maurice Dufrène, creator and director of La Maitrise, also designed products for Saint-Louis crystal and the hardware company Fontaine. Baccarat, measuring the value of its collaboration with Georges Chevalier, doubled its artistic staff. Marcel Goupy, artistic director of the Maison Geo. Rouard, rendered designs for Limoges, La Maitrise, and Saint-Louis, as well. Art-glass master Jean Sala headed Saint-Louis' team of designers.

The English futurist painter, C.R.W. Nevinson, decorated chocolate tins for Cadbury. Surrealist Jean Clement created buttons for Schiaparelli. Christofle produced tableware designed by Jean Cocteau.

In defense of the industrialization of art, Maurice Dufrène wrote, "Without the people, decorative art cannot live." But could the people live without the decorative arts? Advertising assumed an urgent role. Erté, Bérard, Foujita, Icart, Cassandre, Cappiello, Dufy, Dupas and others produced advertisements of such appeal that a new phrase was coined to describe them: commercial art.

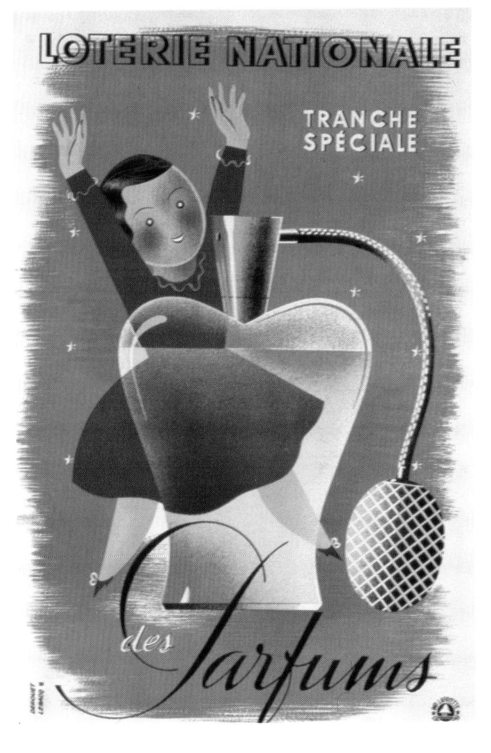

Topaz colored molded and cut-crystal model; flask signed "Tcheco-slovaquie", c.1937. 5.25" X 2.25" diam.

Poster dated 1939, signed "S. Derouet". advertising a special drawing of the French National Lottery. Collection and photo: Bibliothèque Forney, Ville de Paris.

This model's topaz colored, crystal flask was produced in Bohemia for Marcel Franck c.1937. The mount is stamped "Super Fizz". 3.75" X 3.25" X 1.50".

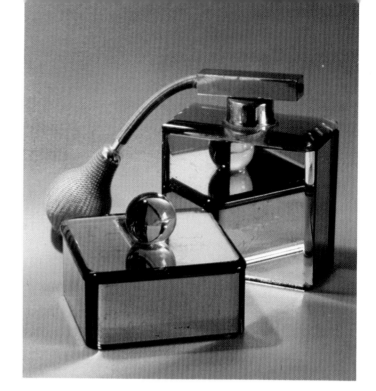

This powder box/atomizer set, panelled with blue-tinted mirrors, reflects a mid-1930's trend in interior decoration.

Bohemian crystal atomizer, c.1937, and matching flask. Atomizer 4.50" X 4" X 2".

Decorators, architects, and engineers searched for common ground upon which to build domestic, commercial, and civic environments which would satisfy the conditions and needs of the future. Marion Dorn, dubbed "the architect of floors", created sculpted carpets and rugs which unified the interiors for which they were designed, serving as liaison between structure and decor. Eileen Gray, under the influence of Le Corbusier, expanded her involvement with furnishings and their context to include the very architecture of the habitat, designing space-efficient dwellings down to the details of the built-in furniture and lighting. Charlotte Perriand and Le Corbusier brainstorm to create "*l'équipement*" which furnished Le Corbusier's "*machines à habiter*". Perriand went on to explore and develop cost-effective building techniques involving modular construction which were to revolutionize modern architecture.

Bohemian malachite glass atomizer with Cupid motif in high relief; late 1930's. 6'' X 2.50'' X 1.50''.

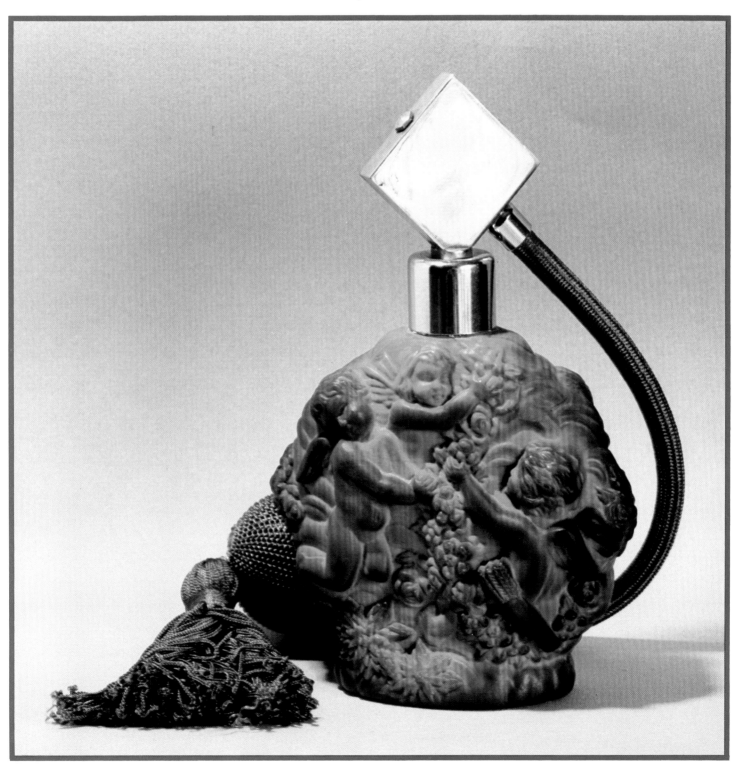

Smoke colored, molded glass model, c. 1937, signed "Tchecoslovaquie". 4" X 3" base diam.

Smoke colored, facet-cut atomizer, c.1937. The mount collar is signed "Sélection Made in France". 5" X 2" X 2".

Smoke colored, cut-crystal atomizer signed "Tcheco-slovaquie", c. 1933. The original chrome has worn off the mount. 2.75" X 3" X 1".

Smoke colored crystal atomizer, c.1933. The mount collar is stamped "Made in France". A sticker on the flask warns, "Never tilt this atomizer in order to use it." 2.50" X 1.75" X 1.75."

Smoke colored, molded and cut crystal atomizer with decor in high relief, signed "Ingrid Czecho-slovakia". c.1937. 5.25" X 2.75" X 2.75."

Crystal atomizer with smoke colored base, c.1937. 4.50" X 2.25" base diam.

Model attributed to DeVilbiss' versatile designer, Frederick Vuillemenot, c.1936. Signed "DeVilbiss Made in U.S.A.". 2.50" X 2.50" X 1".

Even the luxury sector, in apparent contradiction to its nature, was subject to the new imperatives: pragmatism and simplicity. Coco Chanel banked on the concept of the *"non-luxe"*, featuring a collection fashioned of sensible fabrics. The "basic black", a wrinkle-free, jersey dress which swung from the daylight to the starlight look, pivoting on a quick change of accessories, was the mainstay of her collection. While Poiret mocked what he referred to as "Chanel's deluxe poverty", the false modesty of Chanel's fashions and her paste-jewelry accessories (like the cufflinks, buckles, and dress clips, designed for her by Paul Iribe) seemed to strike a chord with her clientele. While Poiret went under, Chanel thrived.

Bohemian uranium glass example, c.1936. Re-mounted with contemporary Marcel Franck mount. 4" X 3.50" X 1.50."

Crystal atomizer with gilded decor. Mount collar stamped "Made in France". c. 1938. 3.75" X 1.75" X 1.75".

Crystal atomizer with black patinated, intaglio decor, c. 1932. 5.50" X 1.50" X 1.50".

Finding the right look, the right image, the right package, the right pitch were now of paramount importance. Expressions like "styling", "re-styling", "dynamic design", "eye appeal", "modernize", peppered the jargon of commerce. The "lay-away plan" and other forms of "sales promotion" were invented, creating consumers for the products which had been created for the consumers. Advertising had become an industry, and industrial design, a serious vocation. The 1930's catch-phrase "design or decline", industry's take-off on the academic adage, "publish or perish", turned out to be equally apt.

Atomizer designed by F.R. Hoch in 1938 for T.J. Holmes Co.—Hoch was the company's vice-president for many years. This example's stream-lined form is typical of American industrial design between the Crash of '29 and the Second World War. The form, a model of aerodynamic principles, was imposed on every-thing from household appliances to tombstones. As the critic John MacArthur put it in 1938, "While streamlined paper cups, if dropped, would fall with less wind resistance, they are no better than the old ones for the purpose for which they are actually intended, namely, drinking." 2.75" X 3.75" X 1".

Scented calling card advertising Piver's "Un Parfum d'Aventure", c.1930.

Bevelled crystal atomizer, French, c.1937. Mount collar originally chrome-plated. 5" X 3" diam.

Frosted blue glass atomizer, c.1935, evoking the image of Josephine Baker; The energy with which this charismatic Blues singer animated her Parisian reviews in the '20s, '30s, and '40s was paralleled only by the energy she invested in her life-long campaign against racism. Collection: Belle de Jour, Montmartre, Paris.

Marcel Goupy and La Maison Geo. Rouard

La Maison Georges Rouard, 34 Avenue de l'Opera, Paris, was a center for the decorative arts in France for fifty years, succeeding important stores like Bing's Galeries de l'Art Nouveau (which had given its name to that style). Beginning in 1900, Georges Rouard, having taken over a ceramics store called "A la Paix," set out to build a new image for French tableware. He called upon a young painter, Marcel Goupy, to join the Maison Rouard as artistic director in 1909. Rouard and Goupy, rejecting the out-dated inventory they had acquired with the shop, stocked up on high-quality decorative and utilitarian ceramics, and glassware which was several steps ahead of contemporary fashion trends.

Rouard was among the first to promote the ceramics of artists like Decoeur, Delaherche, Mayodon, and Lenoble, and to expose the hammered metalwork and lacquerwork of Jean Dunand. More of a gallery than a store, La Maison Geo. Rouard exhibited glassware of exclusive design created for the shop by Lalique, Decorchement, Marinot, Navarre, Schneider, and, in the '20s and '30s, by Marcel Goupy himself. Rouard's display at the l925 exposition was awarded the Grand Prix.

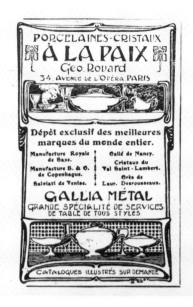

Advertisement from the magazine *L'Art Décoratif*, 1905, for a foundering porcelain and crystal shop named A la Paix, which was resurrected by Georges Rouard.

Advertisement from *Renaissance de l'Art Français et des Industries de Luxe*, 1925, for La Maison Rouard.

By the 1930's, Rouard's glass and ceramics gallery is so well known only the name, logo, and address appear in his ads.

Photograph of enamelled crystal flasks from a *garniture de toilette* designed by Marcel Goupy, published in the magazine *Mobilier et Décoration*, 1925. Collection and photo: Bibliothèque Forney, Ville de Paris.

Garniture de toilette "Deauville" cristal uni,
composée de : 2 flacons, I stilligoutte monture chromée,
I vaporisateur monture chromée, I boîte à poudre, I gobelet 116. »

Garniture de toilette "Monte-Carlo", cristal gravé,
composée de : 2 flacons, I stilligoutte monture chromée,
I vaporisateur monture chromée, I boîte à poudre, I gobelet 158. »

Garniture de toilette "Michelangelo", cristal gravé,
composée de : 2 flacons, I stilligoutte monture dorée,
I vaporisateur monture dorée, I boîte à poudre, I gobelet 261.50

1935 Rouard catalogue representing
a selection of the toilet sets created
for the firm during Marcel Goupy's
tenure as artistic director. Collection
and photo: Bibliothèque Forney,
Ville de Paris.

The "Escale" travel atomizer by
Marcel Franck was created in 1936;
production was discontinued in 1972.
2.75" X 2.50" X 1".

Crystal travel atomizer with mount
signed "Escale Marcel Franck Made
in France", c.1936. 4.25" X 2.25" X
1".

Crystal atomizer by Marcel Franck, c.1932. Collar of mount stamped "Fizz Made in France". 4.50" X 2.75" diam.

Marcel Franck's sophisticated mount "l'Escale," updates the classic, flute-cut travel atomizer. 4.25" X 1.50" diam.

A flyer announcing Marcel Franck's pocket model "Le Super Kid", registered May 22, 1931. Collection: Belle de Jour, Montmartre, Paris.

✣ 109

Thanks to his painter's sense of color and line, Goupy became an outstanding designer and decorator of both glass and ceramics. Goupy's *garnitures de toilette* were generally fashioned of blown cristaline, light and fanciful in form. He had a weakness for Venetian glass, which his work reflected. Goupy's early decoration, colorful and arabesque, was executed in a combination of liquid-looking, translucent and opaque enamels which played with the light.

Georges Rouard died in 1929 and was succeeded by his son in the business. Goupy's role as both artist and director became more significant than ever. Under his eye, the Maison Rouard became one of the legendary design power-houses of the 1930's, along with Dufrène's La Maitrise and Follot's Pomone. The Maison Rouard took the Grand Prix again at the Exposition Coloniale in 1931. Goupy's glassware was of increasingly cubist inspiration as the decade advanced, and there was less of it. Drawn to ceramics, he more or less abandoned glass as a medium around 1940 and devoted his last years to the decoration of pottery and porcelain.

Perfume atomizers designed by Marcel Goupy are very rare. They each were probably created originally as part of a matching toilet set. Pieces from the *garnitures de toilette* Goupy made for the Maison Rouard were sometimes signed in enamel near or on the base. Many of his creations, though, were unsigned, including the toilet sets he made for Saint-Louis and La Maitrise.

In 1931, the year the keel plates were laid for the art-laden, French luxury-liner "Normandie", Marcel Franck launched his deluxe pocket atomizer "Le Super Kid". At 80 francs, more than twice the price of the most expensive "Le Kid", this elegant novelty was, never the less, a success.

Crystal flask signed "Tchecoslovaquie"; mount signed "Sélection Made in France." c.1936. 3" X 2.50" X 1.50".

Crystal atomizer with frosted, intaglio decor. Mount collar signed "Sélection Made in France", 1938. 5" X 2" X 2".

Crystal atomizer with mount collar marked "Sélection Made in France", c.1937. 4" X 2" X 2".

Baccarat atomizers of the "Malmaison" pattern (which, in the case of such accessories, is the same as the pattern called "Harcourt"). The exceptionally high lead content of Baccarat crystal, 32%, accounts for its remarkable light-refractive quality, thus its superior brilliance. Right: 5.50" X 2.50" diam., unsigned, c.1935. Left: 4.75" X 2.25" diam., signed with trademark, c.1960.

1937 Baccarat catalogue featuring a facet-cut toilet set. Collection and photo: Bibliothèque Forney, Ville de Paris.

Guerlain atomizer fashioned of Baccarat crystal with its leather travel case by Hermes. The atomizer's mount is signed "Guerlain", as is the inside of the case's lid. The flask bears the Baccarat trademark. Perfume companies and other atomizer makers often offered the option of such a box, in the tradition of the *nécessaire de toilette*. The *nécessaire* was a portable dressing case outfitted with innumerable utensils and containers for the products and rites associated with a lady's upkeep. Guerlain's 1900 model was one of the first atomizers available in a travel kit format; Later in the century, a number of R. Lalique's atomizers, including the star-studded globe created from Worth's perfume "Dans la Nuit", came with their customized cases; Houbigant's facet-cut atomizer was presented in a sort of velvet-lined jewellers box; and cases were a standard accessory for most of Marcel Franck's travel atomizers. Atomizer 4" X 2" diam.

Guerlain atomizer, c.1935. Bottom of the crystal flask bears the acid-etched Baccarat trademark as well as an engraved number, "34", and "Guerlain". The mount is also signed "Guerlain". This model was fabricated from the mid-1930's to the mid-1960's.

Classic "Boule Baccarat". The mount style suggests that this example dates from the 1930's. There is no signature, as was often the case of Baccarat products fabricated prior to 1936. 4.50" X 3.25 diam.

"Boule Baccarat" with more recent mount style, c.1960. Acid-etched Baccarat logo on bottom of flask. 4" X 3.25" diam.

Crystal atomizer, French, c.1937 4.75" X 3" X 2".

Wide-necked atomizer's atomizer with mount signed "Volupté", c.1932; used as a pump to fill pocket atomizers. 3.25" X 4.50" X 2.50".

A very common 1930's model, found in all the popular colors: Pale blue, pale rose, smoke, topaz, amber, and pale green. 4.25" X 2.25" base diam.

Molded glass atomizer, c.1938. 3'' X
4'' X 1.5''.

Crystal atomizer, Germany, c.1935.
5'' X 3.25'' X 3''.

This molded glass model is pictured in the 1935 catalogue of *nouveautés* of Paris's BHV department store. 4.50" X 3" base diam.

Crystal perfume atomizer, Germany, c.1935. 6" X 4.25" diam.

English cut-glass model, c.1935.

English crystal atomizer, c.1930.
3.50" X 4" X 2".

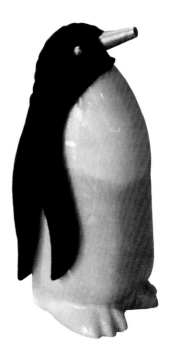

China atomizer in the form of a penguin signed "DeVilbiss" and "Lenox". The black felt tailcoat conceals a recessed rubber bulb which propels a jet of perfume out the penguin's beak. c.1936. approx H.4." Collection: Belle de Jour, Montmartre, Paris.

This porcelain atomizer is one of a series of exotic miniatures made for the souvenir market around the time of the French Exposition Coloniale of 1931. 3" X 1.5" X 1".

Pocket-sized crystal atomizer, c.1930. 2.50" X 1" diam.

Miniature porcelain atomizer, c.1931. 2.50" X 1.50" X -75".

SAINT·LOUIS
FRANCE
1586

Saint-Louis' Designers

Saint-Louis was France's original Cristallerie Royale; its off-spring include Baccarat and Val St. Lambert. The name Saint-Louis dates from 1767, though there has been a glassworks on the Saint-Louis site, in the thick of the forests of the northern Vosges mountains, continuously since 1556. Saint-Louis became the first glasshouse in France to fabricate crystal in 1781.

In the late 19th and early 20th centuries though, Saint-Louis was, territorially speaking, a German company. Keeping pace with the great Bohemian glasshouses, Saint-Louis excelled in the production of agate glass, uranium glass, marble and malachite glass, cobalt, ruby, and emerald cased glass, opalines, gold incrustation and enamelling, filligree... a spectrum of techniques which yielded a dazzling assortment of products. Being located in the Alsace-Lorraine, the *cristallerie* was also subject to the pull of the Art Nouveau movement fomenting in Nancy at the century's end. Saint-Louis' sideline of acid-etched cameo glass, designed primarily by Paul Nicolas and his colleague Mercier, was signed "d'Argental". Both Nicolas and Mercier had been associated with the atelier of Emile Gallé. Saint-Louis' earliest Art Nouveau pieces date from the late 1890's; production continued well into the 1920's.

After the First World War, when the Alsace-Lorraine was restored to France, Saint-Louis rejoined the mainstream of the French decorative arts. In addition to Nicolas and Mercier, the era's most *au courant* designers were invited to rejuvenate the Saint-Louis image.

By 1925, Saint-Louis' products were as sophisticated and innovative as any in France. Marcel Goupy designed a popular line of enamel glass tableware for Saint-Louis as well as *flaconnage* in forms which evoked the Murano glass he admired. Maurice Dufrène created both etched and enamelled products for Saint-Louis, who, reciprocally, executed a series of Dufrène patterns exclusively for his decoration boutique, La Maitrise. Jean Luce generated designs for Saint-Louis and Saint-Louis executed pieces designed by Luce for his proper signature.

Blueprint for a Saint-Louis toilet set, "Taille Biseaux", by Jean Sala, 1935. The atomizer flask (top, center) is unmounted, as is often the case in production drawings. Collection: Cristalleries de Saint-Louis.

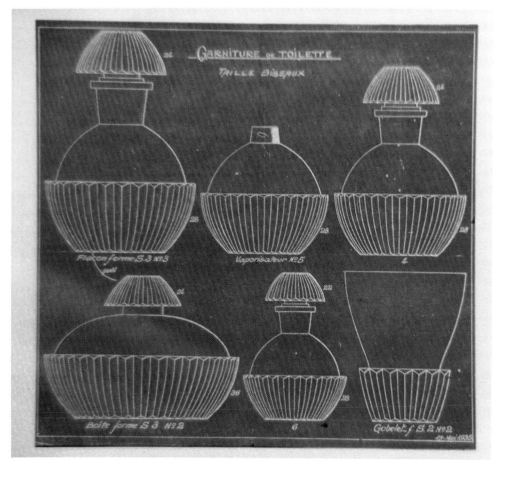

Opposite page top:
One of a series of working sketches for toilet sets designed by Moser of Saint-Louis in 1939. The atomizer flask (center) is represented without its mount. Collection and photo: Cristalleries de Saint-Louis.

Opposite page center:
Toilet set designed by Moser of Saint-Louis, 1939. The decor shown on the flask (left) is not drawn in on the atomizer flask (center) or powder box (right). Collection and photo: Cristalleries de Saint-Louis.

Opposite page bottom:
Toilet set project by Moser for Saint-Louis, 1939. Collection and photo: Cristalleries de Saint-Louis.

GARNITURE DE TOILETTE   Sk 2. M

TAILLE Nº ...... M.

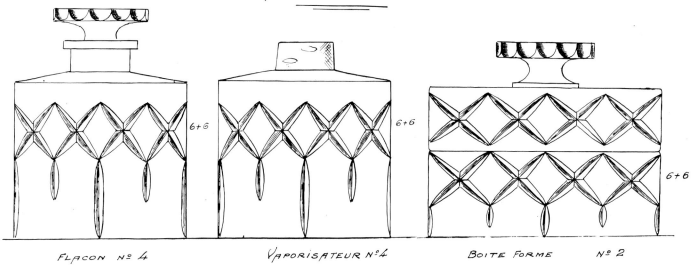

FLACON Nº 4   VAPORISATEUR Nº 4   BOITE FORME   Nº 2

6+6   6+6   6+6

GARNITURE DE TOILETTE   Sk 5. M.

TAILLE Nº ...... M.

7. 8. 1939.

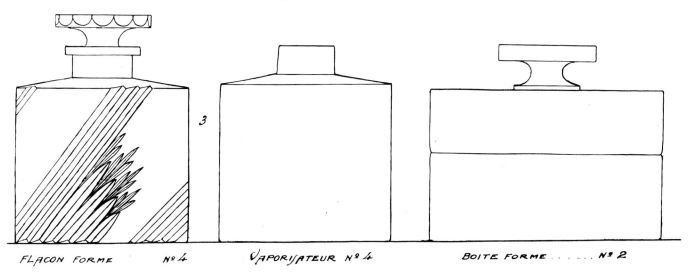

3

FLACON FORME   Nº 4   VAPORISATEUR Nº 4   BOITE FORME ..... Nº 2

GARNITURE DE TOILETTE   Sk. 6. M.

TAILLE Nº ...... M.

FLACON FORME ..... Nº 4   VAPORISATEUR Nº 4   BOITE FORME ...... Nº 2

8 Août 1939

♣ 119

1938 Saint-Louis catalogue picturing a bevel-cut toilet set (top) created by Jean Sala in 1935. While Sala was artistic director at Saint-Louis from 1938 to 1944, his association with the glassworks officially spanned nearly two decades, extending form 1933 until at least 1952. Collection and photo: Bibliothèque Forney, Ville de Paris.

Bevelled crystal atomizer from a toilet set created by Jean Sala for Saint-Louis in 1935.

One of Saint-Louis' most notable collaborators, Jean Sala (artistic director from 1938 to 1944), came from a long line of Catalonian glassblowers and was, himself, a virtuoso in the medium known as malfin glass. Malfin glass, shot through with air bubbles and miscellaneous undigested ingredients which are deliberately not refined out of the molten batch, has a rough, lava-like quality; Sala customarily cased the porous malfin glass in clear glass, forming a light weight but somewhat resilient laminate which he then shaped. Sala was also fascinated by *pâte-de-verre*, another free-spirited material. His art-glass creations had a spontaneous quality, though they undoubtedly required an extravagant amount of time to complete. Each piece was unique.

Atomizer flask with gilded decor designed by Jean Sala for Saint-Louis in 1936. Collection: Cristalleries de Saint-Louis.

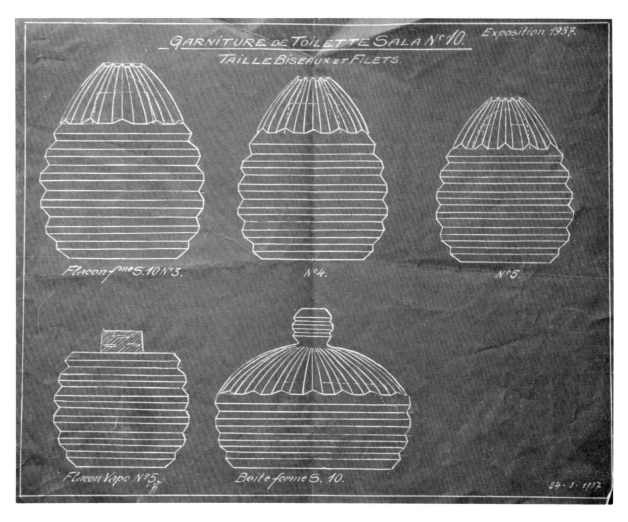

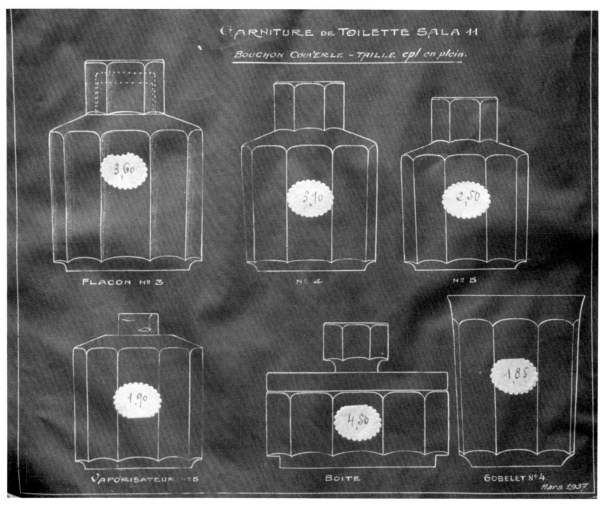

Given Sala's hands-on orientation, it is a credit to his versatility that he was also able to adapt to the role of large-scale production designer for Saint-Louis. In addition. Sala designed commercial perfume bottles for Lancôme, joining René Lalique, and Véronique Monod (who designed for Christian Dior) as one of the rare glass-blower/bottle-designers in the history of the perfume industry.

Atomizers or toilet sets designed for Saint-Louis by Sala, like those created for the firm by Goupy and Dufrène, are not artist-signed.

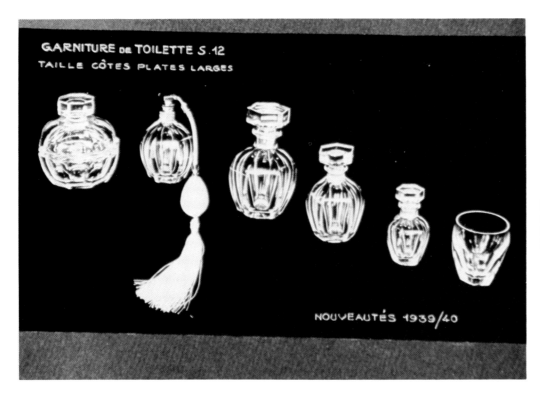

Saint-Louis toilet set "S.12" attributed to Jean Sala, dated 1939. Collection: Cristalleries de Saint-Louis.

Saint-Louis toilet set "S. 17" attributed to Jean Sala, 1939. Collection: Cristalleries de Saint Louis.

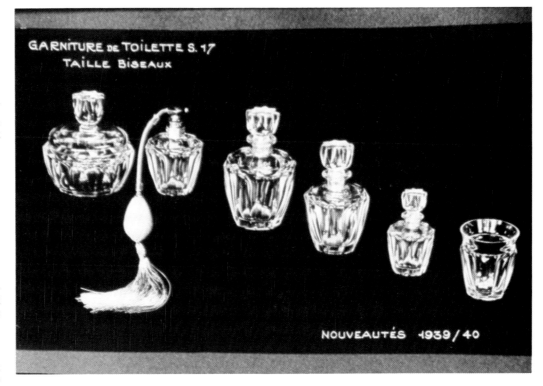

Opposite page top:
Blueprint for a Saint-Louis bevel-cut toilet set, "Sala Nr. 10", dated 1937, by Jean Sala. Collection: Cristalleries de Saint-Louis.

Opposite page bottom:
Blueprint for "Sala 11", a flute-cut toilet set designed by Jean Sala for Saint-Louis in 1937. Collection: Cristalleries de Saint-Louis.

ARTICLES DIVERS　GARNITURES DE TOILETTE

FORME 589 TAILLE Nº 761

FLACON Nº4　　　　Nº5　　　BOITE A POUDRE　　VAPORISATEUR

FORME 589 TAILLE Nº 999

FLACON Nº4　　　　Nº5　　　BOITE A POUDRE　　VAPORISATEUR

FORME S.12 TAILLE C.P.L LARGES

    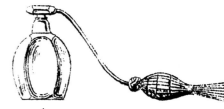

FLACON Nº3　　Nº4　　Nº6　　BOITE A POUDRE　GOB. Nº4　VAPORISATEUR

FORME 583 BIS TAILLE Nº 1027

FLACON Nº3　　　　Nº4　　　BOITE A POUDRE　　VAPORISATEUR

FORME 610 TAILLE Nº 11670

FLACON Nº3　　　　Nº4　　　BOITE A POUDRE　　VAPORISATEUR

Atomizers pictured in Saint-Louis price book from 1939. Collection and photo: Cristalleries de Saint-Louis.

The Garniture de Toilette

Each passing decade of the 20th century took its toll on the *garniture de toilette*. At the turn of the century, a *garniture de toilette* of twenty or more pieces was not uncommon. By the 1930's, even the *garniture* deluxe of Baccarat or Saint-Louis boasted only six pieces: atomizer, powderbox, three flasks, and a goblet. The norm had dwindled to two pieces by the end of the decade: the atomizer and the powder box.

Many of the products associated with a woman's grooming at the turn of the century had disappeared, along with the habits which they implied. The products remaining in use, lotions, toilet waters, perfumes, and powders, were marketed in exquisite containers of their own. The famous Lanvin bottle for "My Sin", known as the "boule noire", with its emblem (designed by Paul Iribe) allegedly depicting Jeanne Lanvin and her daughter, the perfume "Lilas" by Gabilla in its classic Lalique bottle, Chevalier's marvelous perfume flask for the Lubin scent, "L'Océan Bleu", figuring a pair of dolphins, these were products with immense prestige. They were meant to be flaunted, not tamely decanted into a flask in a series of identical flasks, however elegant. The *garniture de toilette* had lost, by the 1930's, its *raison d'être*.

Neither was a woman's life, in 1930, what it had been in 1900. The woman who contributed financially to the support of her family, not to mention herself, had become a middle class phenomenon. Women who married were marrying later and tended to continue to pursue the careers they had established even when it was no longer economically essential. The class of women who had unlimited time to devote to the daily *toilette* was shrinking, as was the space allotted to the ritual's paraphernalia. The gracious dwellings of the Belle Epoque were being broken up into efficiency apartments.

What accounts, then, for the persistent popularity of the toilet set's novice, the perfume atomizer, in the face of this attrition? For one thing, vaporizing a perfume permits a more even and sparing diffusion of the substance. Also, an atomizer protects its costly contents from spillage and evaporation, as well as from exposure (via the fingertip) to body oils or other impurities which might undermine the perfume's chemical stability. However, the atomizer's success cannot be explained in practical terms alone. The object itself has an undeniable magnetism. Once in an atomizer's ken, it is hard to resist the urge to pick it up, squeeze its bulb, and, as turn of the century beauty consultant, Rose Nicolle, put it, "inhale the perfume which rises delicately into your ecstatic nostrils." The perfume atomizer became a sort of feminine fetich, remaining as the privileged token of the traditional *garniture de toilette*.

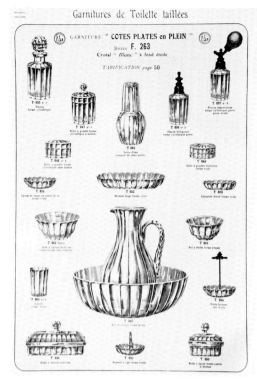

Twenty piece toilet set pictured in the 1916 Baccarat catalogue.

Bohemian crystal powder box and atomizer with engraved and silver decor. Atomizer mount originally chrome-plated. Flask signed "Tchecoslovaquie". c.1935. 3" X 3.50" X 2".

Chapter Four

Conclusion

The institutionalization of industrial design and creative sales promotion, essential to the survival of commerce during the depression years, had some unexpected consequences. What began as a concern for the practical and esthetic superiority of a product, rather quickly degenerated into a preoccupation with "styling", that is, the constant alteration of form and proportion calculated to render the competitor's model (or one's own previous model) obsolete. Because a toaster, a chair, or a car designed to be replaced within the decade need not be constructed to last a lifetime, planned obsolescence soon became a structural phenomenon as well as an esthetic one. The products, less durable, could be manufactured more and more competitively.

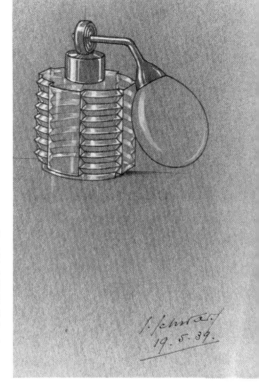

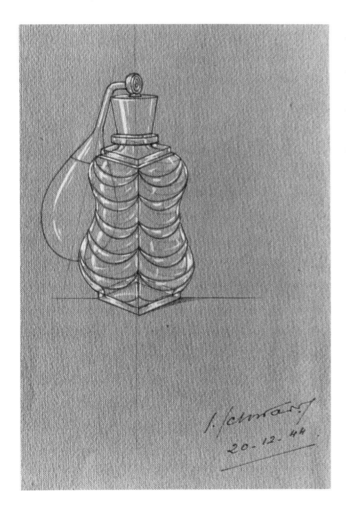

Three designs by Schwander of the Verreries Brosse, from 1939, 1944, and 1950, illustrating the concept of "styling": the art of playing with proportions and combinations of design themes frequently and systematically in order to out-mode previous models without actually disturbing established tastes. Collection: Verreries Brosse, Paris.

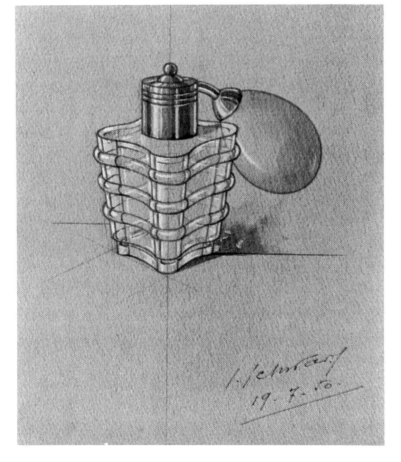

Opposite page:
Crystal atomizer by Val Saint-Lambert, c.1958, bearing hand-etched signature on bottom of flask. (Mount not original.) 6.50" X 2" X 2'

Crystal atomizer designed by F.R. Hoch for T.J. Holmes Co., 1944.

The emergence of plastics, as a result of industrial developments concurrent with the Second World War, accelerated the calculated mortality of merchandise in general. An increasing number of consumer goods were out-right disposable. The atomizer, already suffering an esthetic decline in the late 1930's as a result of the mania for styling, was laid low in the post-war era by the advent of the aerosol spray. It happens that the freon gas used in aerosols, however, violated the chemical integrity of the perfume, affecting its appearance, fragrance, and stamina. The perfume industry (well before freon was identified as a threat to the environment) abandoned the popular aerosol in favor of the low-cost, low-tech, plastic pump spray.

The non-refillable pump sprays with which the bottles of most brands of perfume are equipped today represent a merger of the traditional atomizer with the commercial perfume bottle. This product conforms superbly well to the profile of today's perfume consumer. A woman no longer necessarily identifies with a single fragrance for life. She may wear two or three scents in the course of a week, or change brands altogether several times a year. Since, obviously, perfumes cannot be mixed, and since it is difficult to entirely vanquish an established odor from an atomizer, the integral pump-spray proves convenient. Logically, the spray should long since have supplanted the atomizer altogether.

The atomizer, however, is currently enjoying a revival. Nina Ricci, Lanvin, and Dior, all feature refillable atomizers as exclusive accessories to their fashions and fragrances. Lalique, Baccarat, Daum, and Saint-Louis create and recreate atomizers in the grand tradition; and the firm of Marcel Franck, which celebrated its 100th birthday in 1984, is thriving.

Limoges porcelain poodle atomizer, c.1940, signed "Kitzinger Frères". Collection: Belle de Jour, Montmartre, Paris.

"Le Pacha", a single-handed atomizer advertised as "totally non-mechanical", was fabricated by J. Veissiere of Paris from the early 1940's to the mid-1980's. It was suited to the diffusion of brilliantine, hair lacquer, or talcum powder, as well as eau de toilette.

Black glass atomizer with gilt decor,
c.1945. 2.50'' X 2'' X 2''.

Black glass and gold-plated brass
purse model by ''V.B. Paris''. 3'' X
.75'' diam.

Roja brilliantine was sold in this
atomizer bottle, c.1945. 4.50'' X 2'' X
1.25''.

"Weekend" pocket atomizers by Marcel Franck, c.1948. Collection: Marcel Franck, Paris.

"Le Weekend" was created by Marcel Franck in 1948; the finishes ranged from basic chrome-plate to deluxe snakeskin.

Original atomizer design by Schwander of the Verreries Brosse dated July 7th, 1950. Collection: Verreries Brosse, Paris.

Late-30's styles, such as this facet-cut format, were touched up and re-presented in the late 40's, after a hiatus of nearly a decade owing to the war and its aftermath. 4" X 2" X 2".

This molded "demi-cristal" atomizer, c.1950, is a post-war edition of a pre-war design. The sticker on the flask reads "Vaporisateurs Ch. Cordier Paris". So called demi-cristal or cristalline contains some lead but not the 24% necessary to warrant the description "Lead crystal". Full lead crystal, or *cristal supérieur*, according to standards observed in the European Economic Community, must contain no less than 30% lead. 4.25" X 4.25" X 2".

"Escale" travel atomizer by Marcel Franck in its leather case, c.1950. 3" X 2.50" X 1.75".

Molded glass atomizer with pump mount, France, c.1950. 3.50" X 2.50" diam.

This model, combining late-30's design features, is, however, a post-war product. The flask is signed "Tchechoslovaquie". The flow of Bohemian glassware, which had previously inundated Western Europe, was severely reduced in the post-war era. The quality of the crystal was not always on a parr, either, with pre-war examples. 3.50" X 3.50" diam.

Opposite page:
Travel atomizer with mount signed "Le Provençal Molinard" created for Molinard by Marcel Franck, c.1950. 5" X 2" X 1.75".

FIRCSA

POUR LE VOYAGE

MARCEL FRANCK VOUS CONSEILLE

ESCALE

LE MEILLEUR VAPORISATEUR DU MONDE

Rigoureusement étanche
Fermeture de sécurité

1961 Guerlain catalogue advertising a re-edition of their "1900" model atomizer. Collection and photo: Bibliothèque Forney, Ville de Paris.

One of the marvels on display at the Bon Marché exhibit, "Le Parfum et ses Merveilles", Paris, 1991, was this atomizer in the form of a Chianti bottle created for Schiaparelli's 1957 perfume "Si." The name "Si" was inspired by a Juliette Gréco song of that title which was popular that year; all but one of Schiaparelli's scents begin with the letter "S". The atomizer bottle is fashioned of glass with a gilded and enamelled decor. The bulb, tube, and mount are of gilded metal. Collection: Belle de Jour, Montmartre, Paris.

Opposite page:
1950 ad for the Marcel Franck travel atomizer "Escale".

L'origan

PARFUM · EAU DE COLOGNE · EAU DE TOILETTE · LOTION · BRILLANTINES
POUDRE AIR SPUN · POUDRE DE TOILETTE · TALC · SELS DE BAIN · SAVONS

Original design for a Verreries Brosse project, signed "G. Schwander 5-4-54". Such drawings represented the first phase of the industrial glass-maker's creative process. Once the client selected a design from the drawings presented, a life-sized plaster model was fashioned, which was, in turn, used to make the mold. Collection: Verreries Brosse, Paris.

Opposite page:
1950 ad for Coty's "L'Origan".

Murano blown-glass atomizer, c.1965: A banalized example of a technique exploiting the decorative value of trapped air bubbles which was pioneered as early as 1922 by Maurice Marinot. 3.50" X 2.50" diam.

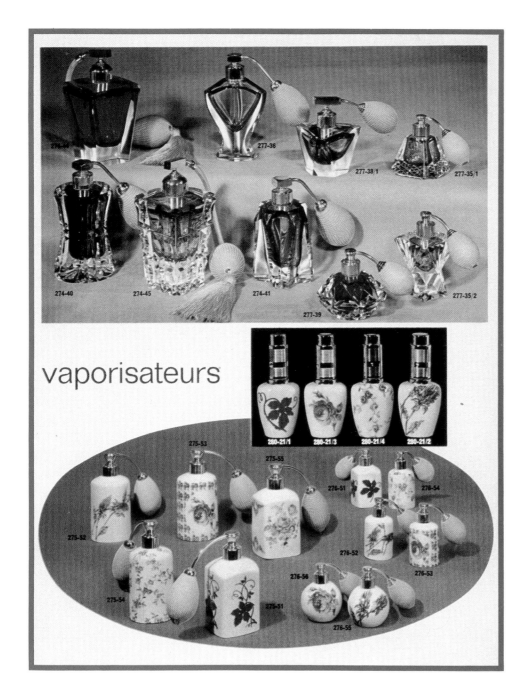

vaporisateurs

1963 Féret Frères catalogue featuring Bohemian *Arc-en-ciel* (rainbow) glass models (top) and various Limoges porcelain models (center & bottom). Collection and photo: Bibliothèque Forney, Ville de Paris.

Gem-cut crystal atomizer, c.1970. 3.75" X 1.25" X 1.25.

Bohemian rainbow glass model, early 1960s. 4.25'' X 2.50'' X 1.50''.

This ceramic Pierrot atomizer charms his audience at the Bon Marché exhibit "Le Parfum et ses Merveilles", Paris, 1991. Collection: Belle de Jour, Montmartre, Paris.

Baccarat crystal atomizer, c.1960. The bottom of the flask bears the acid-etched Baccarat logo picturing a stemmed wine glass, a carafe, and a tumbler. As a rule, pieces produced from 1936 on are signed with this logo.

Crystal atomizer, c.1968, in the free-style form pioneered by Daum. 5.50" X 3" X 3".

Bolero

Pompadour

Dubarry

Toilet sets from a 1967 Saint-Louis catalogue. Collection: Cristalleries de Saint-Louis. Photo: Françoise Flamant.

Baccarat cut-crystal atomizer, c.1968. Baccarat trademark on bottom of flask. 2.50'' X 2.25'' diam.

1968 Daum catalogue. This limpid crystal atomizer and flask exemplify the contemporary Daum style; the forms may vary from year to year but the purity and beauty of the material are Daum constants. Collection and photo: Bibliothèque Forney, Ville de Paris.

♣ 141

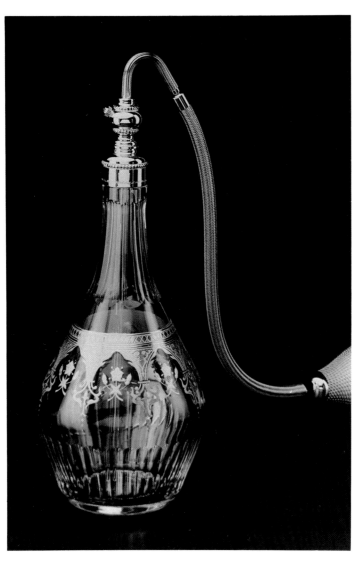

Marcel Franck model, c.1970. The heavy outer formation of clear crystal encases a film of opalescent glass which gives the object an inner glow. 5" X 1.75' X 1.75"

This Saint-Louis opaline atomizer, "Calla", created by Claude Bromet in 1988, keeps faith with tradition while keeping pace with the times. Collection and photo: Cristalleries de Saint-Louis.

Marcel Franck's limited edition, centennial model, created in 1984 by Baccarat, a collector's item from the outset. Collection and photo: Marcel Franck, Paris.

Contemporary purse model by Marcel Franck.

The come-back of the atomizer began with the revival of pre-war styles. More than nostalgia, this revival is also an acknowledgement of the vision shared by William Morris, Emile Gallé, Louis Comfort Tiffany, The Glasgow Four, Candace Wheeler, Kolo Moser, Sonia Delaunay, Paul Poiret and the Martines, Gunta Stölzl, Raoul Dufy, Marianne Brandt, Jean Dunand, Sophie Taeuber-Arp, René Lalique, Eileen Gray, Georges Chevalier, and the thousands of other artists and artisans whose concern for the objective context of daily life contributed to the democratization of art which we may now take for granted.

According to Dorothy Wright Liebes, in her introduction to the catalogue for the 1939 San Francisco World's Fair, "The artistic spirit of an era can be measured by the creative vitality of its every-day objects." If this is so, then the atomizer certainly stands out among the objects by which the creativity of the early 20th century could be measured. And, perhaps, it shall stand out again as the century ends.

1984 Guerlain pocket atomizer with replaceable inner flask, made for "Vol de Nuit".

Intimate treasures of the past presently ornament the shelves of one of Paris' most extraordinary galleries, Régine de Robien's Beauté Divine.

Detail of René Lalique's "Figurines
et Guirlandes" atomizer, c.1925.
Copyright © 1992 ARS, N.Y.
/SPADEM.

Catalogues

From La Belle Epoque

Comptoir de Parfumerie

EXTRAIT pour mouchoir et dentelle, parfums assortis.
Le flacon . . ».95

BOITE A POUDRE en laque du Japon, décors variés, avec la houppe.
Prix. . . . . ».45

VAPORISATEUR en cristal décoré, monture métal nickelé, a balles.
Prix. 1.75

SAVON aux fleurs du Japon.
La boite de trois pains . . . 1.45

CORBEILLE en vannerie fine contenant 12 savons fins assortis.
Prix. 2.60

POUDRE DE RIZ parfum russe. La boite de 100 grammes. . 2.25
Blanche, rose, Rachel.

SACHET PARFUMÉ en satin peint ciel, rose, crème, bouquet varié.
Prix 2.90. 4.90. et 6.90

AFFAIRE
Exceptionnelle
—
EAU DE COLOGNE
POUR LA
TOILETTE

Le flacon litre . . **3.75**
Le flacon 1/2 litre. **1.90**

FLACON ÉCHANTILLON

EAU DE TOILETTE

PARIS-PRINTEMPS

Qui sera offert

gratuitement

à tout acheteur

de parfumerie

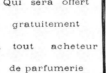

Imprimerie CHAIX (Ateliers Chéret), 20, Bergère, 20, Paris. — 632-1-93. — (Encre Lorilleux).
Le Gérant : STANISLAS EUGÈNE.

1893 Printemps catalogue. Collection and photo: Bibliothèque Forney, Ville de Paris.

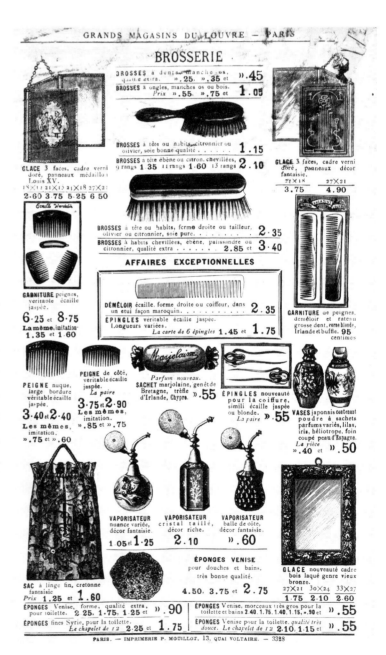

1902 Grands Magasins du Louvre catalogue. Collection and photo: Bibliothèque Forney, Ville de Paris.

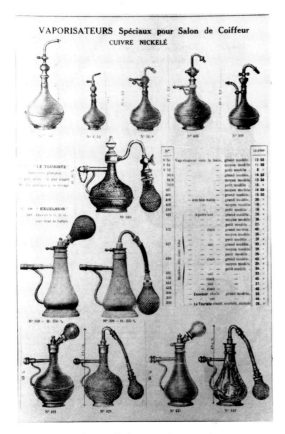

Page from Kitzinger Frères catalogue picturing nickel-plated copper and brass atomizers designed especially for barbers and hairdressers. Collection Belle de Jour, Montmartre, Paris.

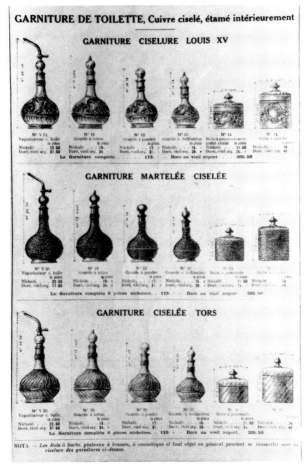

A selection of men's toilet sets in nickel, silver, or gold-plated copper featured in an early Kitzinger Frères catalogue. Collection: Belle de Jour, Montmartre, Paris.

1909 Printemps catalogue. Collection and photo: Bibliothèque Forney, Ville de Paris.

COMPTOIR de BROSSERIE

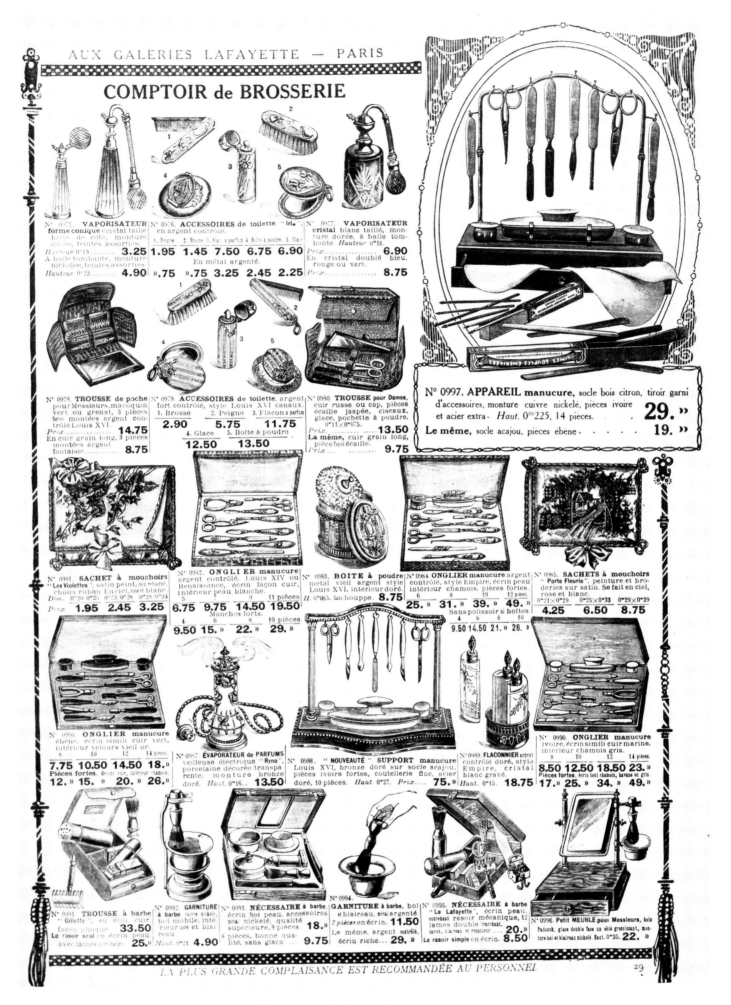

N° 0971. **VAPORISATEUR** forme conique cristal taillé taille de côté, monture dorée, teintes assorties.
Hauteur 0"19......... **3.25**
À balle tombante, monture nickelée, teintes assorties.
Hauteur 0"23........ **4.90**

N° 0976. **ACCESSOIRES** de toilette "Iris" en argent contrôlé.
1. Peigne   2. Brosse 3. Flac. à parfum 4. Boîte à poudre. 5. Glace
1.95   1.45   7.50   6.75   6.90
En métal argenté.
».75   ».75   3.25   2.45   2.25

N° 0977. **VAPORISATEUR** cristal blanc taillé, monture dorée, à balle tombante. Hauteur 0"18.
Prix.............. **6.90**
En cristal doublé bleu, rouge ou vert.
Prix.............. **8.75**

N° 0978. **TROUSSE** de poche pour Messieurs, maroquin vert ou grenat, 3 pièces forts montées argent contrôlé Louis XVI.
Prix.......... **14.75**
En cuir grain long, 3 pièces montées argent fantaisie.......... **8.75**

N° 0979. **ACCESSOIRES** de toilette, argent fort contrôlé, style Louis XVI canaux.
1. Brosse   2. Peigne   3. Flacon à parfum
2.90   5.75   11.75
4. Glace   5. Boîte à poudre
12.50   13.50

N° 0980. **TROUSSE** pour Dames, cuir russe ou cap, pièces écaille jaspée, ciseaux, glace, pochette à poudre. 0"11×0"075.
Prix.......... **13.50**
La même, cuir grain long, pièce façon écaille.
Prix.......... **9.75**

N° 0981. **SACHET** à mouchoirs "Les Violettes", satin peint, nœud ruban, choux ruban. En ciel, rose et blanc. Dim. 0"20 0"25 0"23 0"28 0"25 0"34
Prix... **1.95   2.45   3.25**

N° 0982. **ONGLIER** manucure argent contrôlé, Louis XIV ou Renaissance, écrin façon cuir, intérieur peau blanche.
5   9   11 pièces
6.75   9.75   14.50   19.50
Manches forts.
4   6   8   10 pièces
9.50   15.»   22.»   29.»

N° 0983. **BOITE** à poudre métal vieil argent style Louis XVI, intérieur doré. H. 0"055. Sans houppe. **8.75**

N° 0984. **ONGLIER** manucure argent contrôlé, style Empire, écrin peau intérieur chamois, pièces fortes.
6   8   10   12 pièces
25.»   31.»   39.»   49.»
Sans polissoir ni boîtes.
4   6   8   10
9.50   14.50   21.»   26.»

N° 0985. **SACHETS** à mouchoirs "Porte Fleurie", peinture et broderies sur satin. Se fait en ciel, rose et blanc.
0"21×0"29   0"25×0"33   0"29×0"39
4.25   6.50   8.75

N° 0986. **ONGLIER** manucure ébène, écrin simili cuir vert, intérieur velours vieil or.
8   10   12   14 pièces
7.75   10.50   14.50   18.»
Pièces fortes, écrin cuir, intérieur chamois.
12.»   15.»   20.»   26.»

N° 0987. **ÉVAPORATEUR** de PARFUMS veilleuse électrique "Ryno", porcelaine décorée transparente, monture bronze doré. Haut. 0"16.. **13.50**

N° 0988. "**NOUVEAUTÉ**" **SUPPORT** manucure Louis XVI, bronze doré sur socle acajou, pièces ivoire fortes, coutellerie fine, acier doré, 10 pièces. Haut. 0"27. Prix.... **75.»**

N° 0989. **FLACONNIER** argent contrôlé doré, style Empire, cristal blanc gravé. Haut. 0"15. **18.75**

N° 0990. **ONGLIER** manucure ivoire, écrin simili cuir marine, intérieur chamois gris.
8   10   12   14 pièces
8.50   12.50   18.50   23.»
Pièces fortes, écrin toct chamois, lavable ou gris.
17.»   25.»   34.»   49.»

N° 0991. **TROUSSE** à barbe "Gillette", en étui cuir, façon phoque.......... **33.50**
Le rasoir seul en écrin peau, avec lames de rechange. **25.»**

N° 0992. **GARNITURE** à barbe cuivre nickelé, bol mobile, intérieur cœur et blaireau. Haut. 0"21 **4.90**

N° 0993. **NÉCESSAIRE** à barbe, écrin façon peau, accessoires métal nickelé, qualité supérieure, 9 pièces. **18.»**
8 pièces, bonne qualité, sans glace.... **9.75**

N° 0994. **GARNITURE** à barbe, bol et blaireau, métal argenté.
2 pièces en écrin. **11.50**
Le même, argent contrôlé, écrin riche... **29.»**

N° 0995. **NÉCESSAIRE** à barbe "Le Lafayette", écrin peau, contenant rasoir mécanique, 12 lames double tranchant, savon, blaireau et repasseur.... **20.»**
Le rasoir simple en écrin. **8.50**

N° 0996. Petit **MEUBLE** pour Messieurs, bois Padouck, glace double face et côté grossissant, monture bol et blaireau nickelé. Haut. 0"35. **22.»**

N° 0997. **APPAREIL** manucure, socle bois citron, tiroir garni d'accessoires, monture cuivre nickelé, pièces ivoire et acier extra. Haut. 0m225, 14 pièces. **29.»**
Le même, socle acajou, pièces ébène. **19.»**

1913 Galeries Lafayette department store catalogue. Collection and photo: Bibliothèque Forney, Ville de Paris.

✤ 147

Commercial catalogues from the war era are rare. This 1917 Printemps catalogue introduced the safety razor, packaged in a compact case which also contained a strop and extra blades; it was a practical gift for the soldier at the front. Collection and photo: Bibliothèque Forney, Ville de Paris.

1909 Printemps catalogue. Collection and photo: Bibliothèque Forney, Ville de Paris.

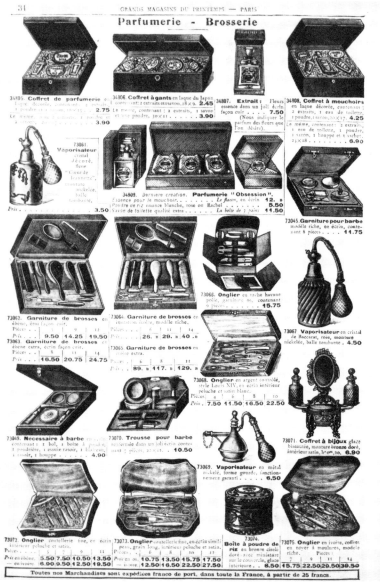

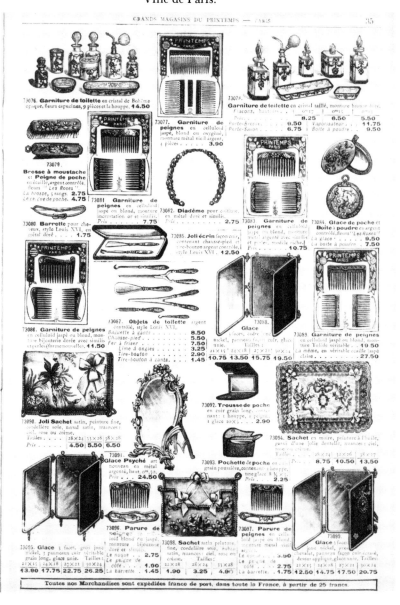

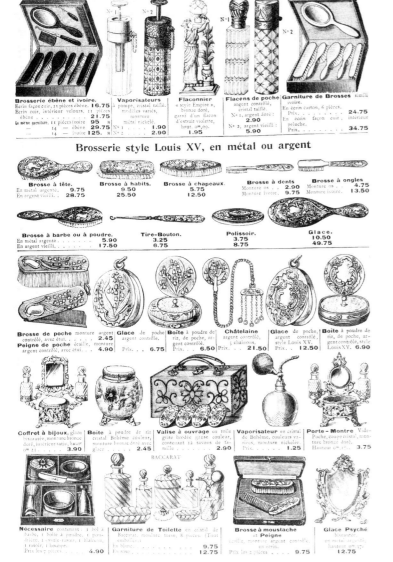

1905 Printemps department store catalogue. Collection and photo: Biblithèque Forney, Ville de Paris.

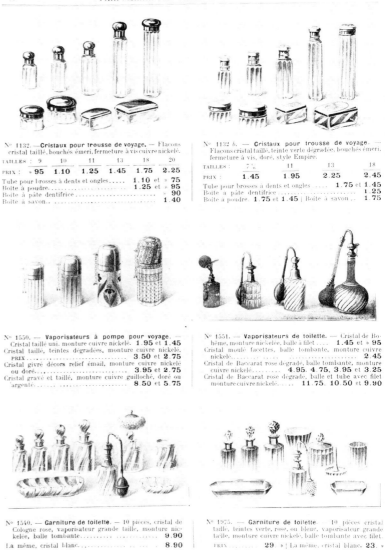

1908 Galeries Saint-Martin department store catalogue. Collection and photo: Bibliothèque Forney, Ville de Paris

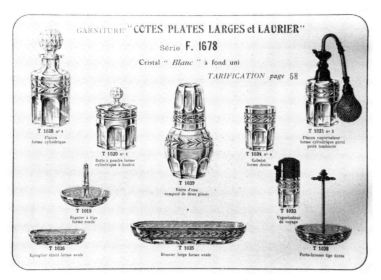

1916 Baccarat catalogue picturing a toilet set in a flute-cut pattern described as "cotes plates larges et Laurier".

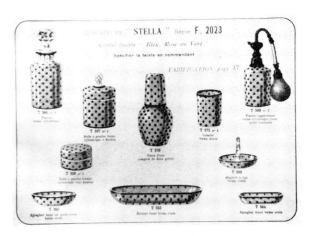

"Stella", a pattern executed in acid-etched cased glass, illustrated in Baccarat's 1916 catalogue.

COMPTOIR ✦ BROSSERIE

N° 0952. CHIFFRE argent, relief ou incrusté pour brosserie ébène, celluloid ou ivoire.

Haut.	1 lettre	2 lettres
0"02	1.50	2.75
0"03	2.25	3.75
0"04	2.95	4.75

N° 0951. BROSSERIE ébène qualité extra.

La brosse :		
Brosse à tête	12 rangs	5.75
— à habits	10	6.25
— à chapeaux	6	2.25
— à poudre	6	1.60
Glace. Largeur 0"10		4.75

N° 0953. BROSSERIE façon ivoire, épaisseur 0"010, choix supérieur.

Brosse à tête	13 rangs	8.25
— à habits	10	7.50
— à chapeaux	6	3.25
— à poudre		2.90
Glace. Largeur 0"10		6.75

N° 0955. GRAVURE pour Brosserie ivoire, métal ou argent.

Haut.	1 lettre	2 lettres
0"02	.75	1.50
0"03	1.25	2.25
0"04	1.75	2.75

N° 0954. BROSSERIE ivoire extra, épaisseur 0"007, soies supérieures. La brosse :

A tête	11 rangs	19.75	A chapeaux	6 rangs	8.75
A habits	9	18.75	A poudre	7	9.50
Glace. Largeur 0"09		26			

N° 0956. BROSSERIE écaille jaspée moulée sur corne. La brosse :

A tête	15 rangs	27.	A chapeaux	7 rangs	12.75
A habits	11	24.	A poudre	8	11.50
Glace. Largeur 0"11		49.			

N° 0974. GARNITURE de toilette cristal de Baccarat, moulure laurier, composée de 10 pièces emballées.

En blanc . **12.50** | En rouge dégradé. **15.75**

N° 0957. BROSSERIE Louis XVI ruban, soies extra.

	Argent	Métal
Brosse à tête	32.	10.50
— à habits	27.	9.75
— à chapeaux droite	18.	7.50
— à poudre	21.	6.25
Glace, largeur 0"10	59.	11.50

N° 0958. GARNITURE toilette cristal blanc, Louis XVI ruban.

	Argent	Métal
Grand flacon	19.50	8.75
Moyen	16.50	7.25
Petit	14.50	6.50
Boîte à poudre	22.	6.50
— à pâte	16.50	4.90

N° 0959. BROSSERIE orfèvre, godrons Louis XIV.

	Argent	Métal
Brosse à tête	55.	31.
— à habits	44.	26.
— à chapeaux	24.	14.
— à poudre	32.	18.
Glace, largeur 0"11	68.	30.

N° 0960. GARNITURE toilette cristal blanc gravé godrons Louis XIV.

	Argent	Métal
Grand flacon	40.	24.
Moyen	33.	21.
Petit	28.	19.
Boîte à poudre	44.	24.
— à pâte	26	15.50

N° 0961. GLACE 3 faces, cadre fort jonc nickelé, panneaux lavables, glaces de choix unies.

0"24	0"18 0"27	0"21 0"30	0"24 0"33 9"2
7.90	9.75	12.75	16.50

N° 0962. GARNITURE brosserie ébène, soies supérieures, en écrin.

Pièces	7	9	12	15
Prix	19.	22.	33.	38.

Même composition en façon ivoire.

| Prix | 24. | 29. | 41. | 52. |

N° 0963. "Psyché". GLACE biseautée, sans monture apparente, fond chevalet acajou.

Dimens.	0"36×0"27	0"42×0"30
Prix	9.50	10.75

N° 0964. GARNITURE brosserie façon ivoire, épaisseur 0"010, soie extra, en écrin riche

Pièces	6	8	10
Prix	42.	49.	56.

Même composition, en ébène extra.

| Prix | 32. | 37. | 43. |

N° 0965. GLACE 3 faces "La Solide", cadre jonc nickelé, panneaux loretd lavables, glaces de choix unies.

0"24	0"18 0"27	0"21 0"30	0"24 0"33 0"27
12.50	14.50	16.	19.

N° 0966. GARNITURE toilette cristal blanc de Baccarat taille Nancy, bouchons facettes, 10 pièces emballées . . **21.**
La même, doubles filets dorés **30.**

N° 0967. VAPORISATEUR pompe cristal blanc gravé, monture métal doré ciselé "Les Liserons"
Haut. 0"09 **4.50** | Haut. 0"10 **5.50**

N° 0968. GLACE 3 faces format homme "Idéale", charnières réglables, cadre fort jonc nickelé, panneaux tekko, glaces St-Gobain unies.

Dimens.	0"21×0"27	0"24×0"30	0"27×0"33
Prix	17.	19.	23.

N° 0969. VAPORISATEUR pompe cristal blanc gravé, monture ciselée, argent contrôlé Louis II, intérieur métal blanc.
Haut. 0"09 **18.** | Haut 0"10 **23.**

N° 0970. GARNITURE de toilette cristal blanc moiré, de "St-Louis", filets dorés, bouchons facettes, 10 pièces emballées. Prix . . . **39.**

Garnitures de Toilette moulées

GARNITURE Série **"BAMBOUS TORS"**

Cristal *"Blanc"*

Forme *"Boule"* TARIFICATION pages 1, 2, 3 et 4

Molded crystal toilet set in the popular "Bambous Tors" pattern, shown in Baccarat's 1916 catalogue. In the late 1880's, a pump capable of blowing glass into its mold was invented; simultaneously, molds which could be assembled from a number of interlinking pieces were being developed. These innovations permitted, for the first time, the mass production of molded crystal and glass objects of some complexity. By the turn of the century, both Baccarat and Saint-Louis had invested in technology.

Molded crystal toilet set in Baccarat's "Serpentine" pattern, 1916 catalogue.

Molded crystal toilet set in the "Laurier" pattern, Baccarat catalogue, 1916.

Opposite page:
1913 Galeries Lafayette catalogue, featuring molded crystal and cut crystal toilet sets by Baccarat and a satin glass toilet set by Saint-Louis. Collection and photo: Bibliothèque Forney, Ville de Paris.

♣ 151

Molded crystal toilet set in the "Russe" pattern from Baccarat's 1916 catalogue.

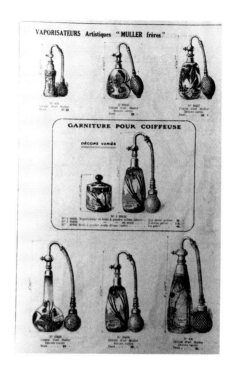

Early Kitzinger Frères catalogue figuring atomizers by Muller Frères. Muller Frères, actually nine brothers and a sister, produced art glass in the style of l'Ecole de Nancy from about 1900 until 1936. Several of the brothers apprenticed in Nancy with Emile Gallé before establishing the family business in nearby Luneville. Collection: Belle de Jour, Montmartre, Paris.

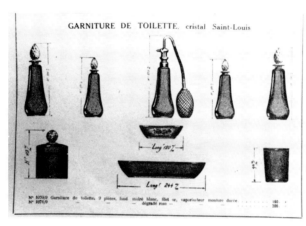

Saint-Louis satin glass toilet set offered in uncolored or graduated, ruby-red crystal by Kitzinger Frères. Collection: Belle de Jour, Montmartre, Paris.

Page from Marcel Franck's 1924 catalogue picturing Saint-Louis satin glass models with gilded motifs in the Louis XVI and Empire styles. These were standard Saint-Louis patterns from the late 19th century through the 1920's. Collection: Belle de Jour, Montmartre, Paris.

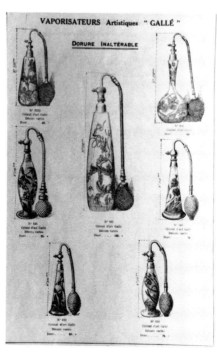

Cameo glass atomizers signed "Gallé" advertised in an early Kitzinger Frères catalogue. Collection: Belle de Jour, Montmartre, Paris.

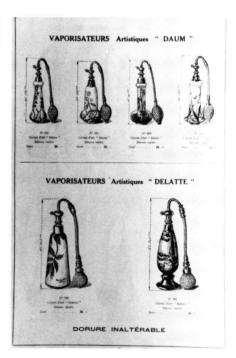

Atomizers signed "Daum" and "Delatte" featured in an early Kitzinger Frères catalogue. Collection: Belle de Jour, Montmartre, Paris.

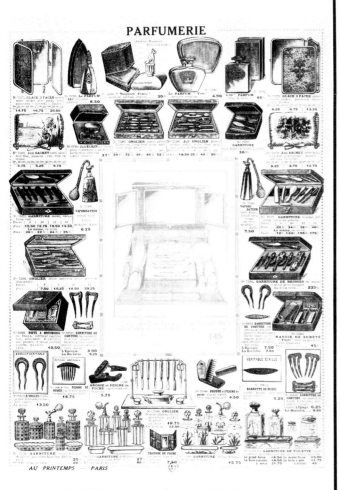

1922 Printemps catalogue. Collection and photo: Bibliothèque Forney, Ville de Paris.

Catalogues from the Art Deco Era

1924-25 Printemps catalogue. Collection and photo: Bibliothèque Forney, Ville de Paris.

Aux illustrations que nous venons de vous présenter, il manque évidemment... la couleur, et, l'espace restreint de ce petit Catalogue, nous empêche de vous soumettre intégralement toute la gamme de nos modèles; cependant, faites-nous l'honneur d'une visite, vous choisirez tout à votre aise les formes et les teintes qui répondent à votre goût.

NOUS POSSÉDONS UN CHOIX UNIQUE A LYON DE VAPORISATEURS

En Cristal de Baccarat — Cristal de Saint-Louis — Cristal de Bohême
et des Modèles inédits de GALLÉ et de ROBJ

...Certainement un Vaporisateur, présenté en coffret, semble plus précieux.

Nous en possédons également un choix varié dont voici trois types :

COFFRETS

Comportant 1 vaporisateur et 1 boîte à poudre portant les meilleures signatures

RB 1015 N, blanc, nickelé	29.50
RB 1015 D, blanc, doré	45. »
RB 1115 D, couleur, doré	51. »

Coffret W 2802 — **80** fr.

contenant :
1 vaporisateur, 1 boîte à poudre
en double cristal marbré,
teintes vives.

Coffret W 2801 — **90** fr.

contenant :
1 vaporisateur grand modèle,
1 boîte à poudre grand modèle
en double cristal marbré,
teintes vives.

1927 Parfumerie Briau, Lyon, catalogue advertising atomizer/powder box gift sets; "...Certainly an atomizer presented in its own special chest seems more precious..." Collection and photo: Bibliothèque Forney, Ville de Paris.

1927 Briau catalogue. Collection and photo: Bibliothèque Forney, Ville de Paris.

Que pensez-vous de cette idée ? Offrir un Vaporisateur ?

Nous en possédons plusieurs milliers en Magasin, tous plus ravissants les uns que les autres ; de toutes les formes et de tous les prix, mais dont nous garantissons le bon fonctionnement.

(Voyez d'ailleurs ces quelques modèles...)

| K 1 - 13.50 | K 2 - 13.59 | K 3 - 13.50 | K 1087 - 14 fr. | K 1088 - 15 fr. | RB 153 - 39.90 |

Nous exécutons toutes les Réparations de Vaporisateurs dans le plus bref délai et aux meilleures conditions.

| MF 2796 - 19.60 | MF 2492 - 18.90 | MF 2882 - 29.50 | MF 2814 - 24.50 | MF 3092 - 24.50 | MF 2541 - 36.50 | MF 2897 - 30.50 |

| RB 04/15 - 13.50 | RB 04/16 - 13.50 | RB 93 - 35 fr. | RB 4/34 - 18.25 | VC 65 - 14.25 | VC 52 - 15.75 | VC 51 - 17.50 | VC 60 - 19.50 |
| RB 115 - 32.90 | RB 4/16 - 18.25 | | RB 04/34 - 13.50 | | | | |

1924 Printemps catalogue. Collection and photo: Bibliothèque Forney, Ville de Paris.

Enamelled glass atomizers created by Quenvil (left & right) and Argy-Rousseau (center) for Marcel Franck, 1924. Collection: Belle de Jour, Montmartre, Paris.

Marcel Franck's 1924 catalogue picturing enamelled glass atomizers signed "Quenvil". Collection: Belle de Jour, Montmartre, Paris.

Argy-Rousseau's "Parrots", Quenvil's "Fuchsias", and Penaud's "Marine" motifs executed in enamel for Marcel Franck's 1924 collection. Collection: Belle de Jour, Montmartre, Paris.

1927 Parfumerie Briau, Lyon, catalogue. The toilet set described as "Garniture VF" (top, left) is an industrial *pâte-de-verre* product of Schneider's subsidiary, Le Verre Français. Collection and photo: Bibliothèque Forney, Ville de Paris.

Baccarat crystal in wheel-cut, cased glass patterns executed for Marcel Franck, l924. Collection: Belle de Jour, Montmartre, Paris.

Cover of Marcel Franck's catalogue or 1924. Collection: Belle de Jour, Montmartre, Paris.

Porcelain atomizers from 1924 Marcel Franck catalogue. Collection: Belle de Jour, Montmartre, Paris.

Instructions for "Le Kid". Collection: Belle de Jour, Montmartre, Paris.

The back page of the 1924 Marcel Franck catalogue reads, "The atomizer is a useful device. The Franck atomizer is a precious ornament." Collection: Belle de Jour, Montmartre, Paris.

... Un tout petit Vaporisateur, pour le sac ou la poche ...

Le "KID"

Son fonctionnement est absolument garanti et parfait.

Sa solidité ne nuit en rien à sa suprême élégance.

Une gamme de nombreux modèles permet de satisfaire tous les goûts et le met à la portée de toutes les bourses.

Au bal, en ville, chez elle, il est indispensable à l'élégante soucieuse d'affirmer son goût raffiné

❖ ❖ ❖

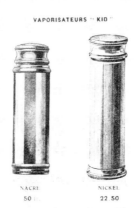

Advertisement for Marcel Franck's "Le Kid" in the l927 Briau catalogue. "Its sturdiness," the ad affirms, "doesn't detract in the least from its supreme elegance." Collection and photo: Bibliothèque Forney, Ville de Paris.

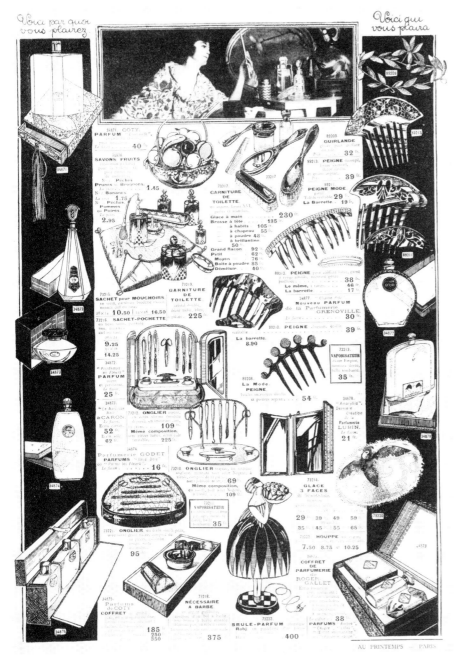

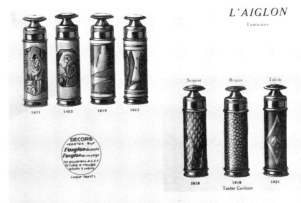

"Fantasies" from the "Aiglon" catalogue, 1929. Collection: Belle de Jour, Montmartre, Paris.

1923 Printemps catalogue picturing an electric perfume burner by Robj, a laurel leaf tiara, a selection of tortoise shell combs, a swan's-down powder puff, along with other trappings of the era. Collection and photo: Bibliothèque Forney, Ville de Paris.

1929 catalogue picturing "l'Aiglon"
models finished in various plastics:
galalith, rhodoid, and nacrolaque.
Collection: Belle de Jour, Montmartre, Paris.

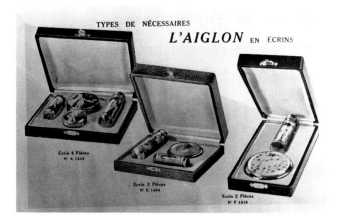

Page from "l'Aiglon" catalogue,
1929, illustrating matching sets whose
elements include the pocket atomizer,
compact, lipstick tube, and cold
cream box. Collection: Belle de Jour,
Montmartre, Paris.

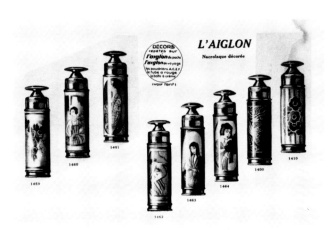

Nacrolaque models from the
"Aiglon" catalogue of 1929.
Collection: Belle de Jour, Mont-
martre, Paris.

Mother-of-pearl models presented in
"l'Aiglon" catalogue, 1929.
Collection: Belle de Jour, Montmartre, Paris.

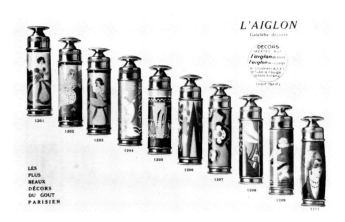

Galalith models from 1929
"l'Aiglon" catalogue. Collection:
Belle de Jour, Montmartre, Paris.

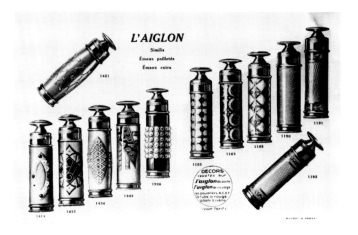

Enamelled models from "l'Aiglon"
catalogue, 1929. Collection: Belle de
Jour, Montmartre, Paris.

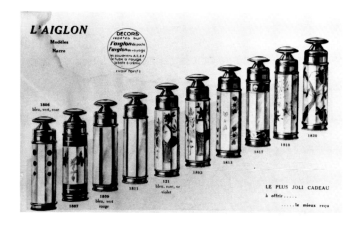

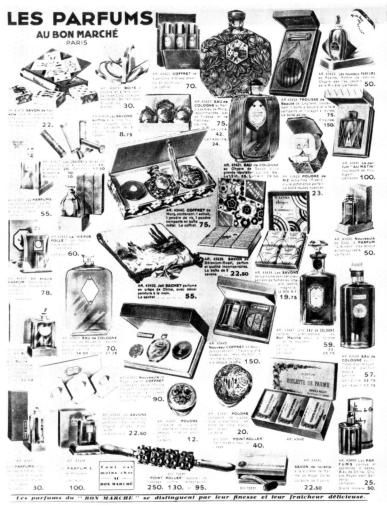

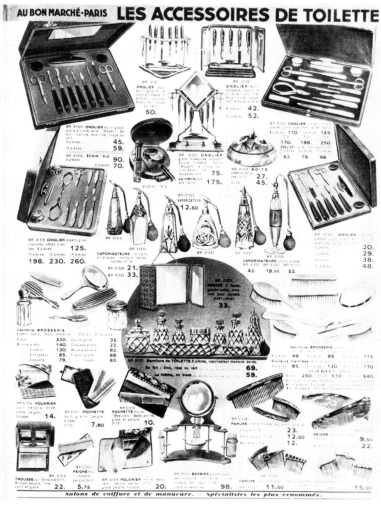

1929 Bon Marché department store catalogue. Collection and photo: Bibliothèque Forney, Ville de Paris.

Porcelain powder boxes, atomizers, and electric perfume burners presented by Kitzinger Frères, in their catalogue c.1922. Collection: Belle de Jour, Montmartre, Paris.

Purse-sized atomizers signed "Paradis" featured in a Kitzinger Frères catalogue, c.1922. Kitzinger Frères also promoted a line of cameo glass atomizers bearing the signature "Paradis". Collection: Belle de Jour, Montmartre, Paris.

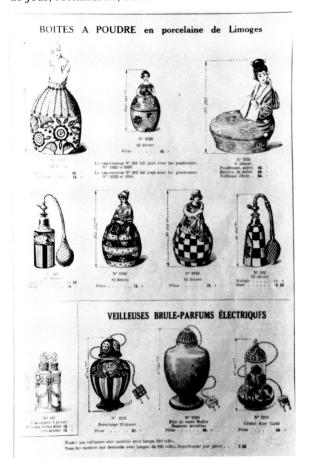

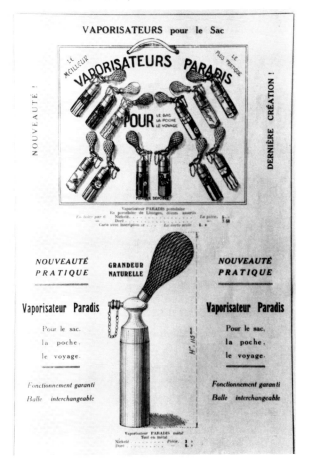

COIFFURE BROSSERIE

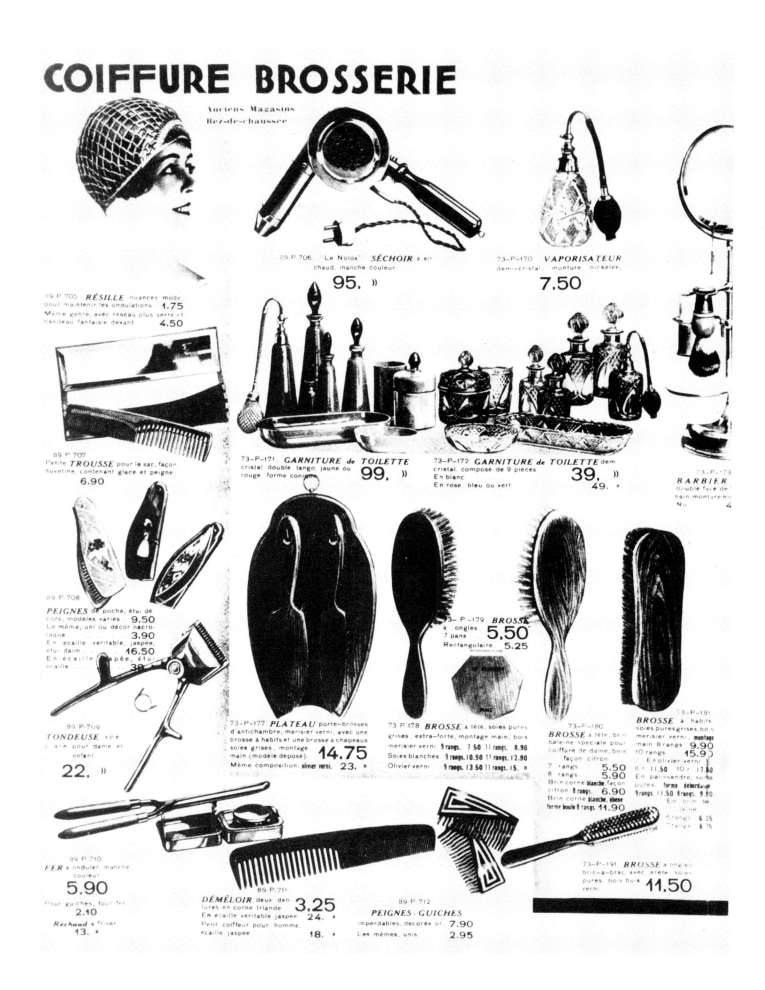

89-P-706. "Le Notos". SÉCHOIR à air
chaud, manche couleur

95. »

73-P-170. VAPORISATEUR
demi-cristal, monture nickelée.

7.50

89-P-705. RÉSILLE nuances mode,
pour maintenir les ondulations **1.75**
Même genre, avec réseau plus serré et
bandeau fantaisie devant **4.50**

89 P 707.
Petite TROUSSE pour le sac, façon
duvetine, contenant glace et peigne
6.90

73-P-171 GARNITURE de TOILETTE
cristal double, tango, jaune ou
rouge, forme conique **99.** »

73-P-172 GARNITURE de TOILETTE dem
cristal, composé de 9 pièces
En blanc **39.** »
En rose, bleu ou vert **49.** »

73-P-173
BARBIER
double face de
bain, monture ni
Nu **4**

89-P-708.
PEIGNES de poche, étui de
core, modèles variés **9.50**
Le même, uni ou décor nacrolaque **3.90**
En écaille véritable, jaspée,
étui daim **16.50**
En écaille jaspée, étui
écaille **39**

73-P-177 PLATEAU porte-brosses
d'antichambre, merisier verni, avec une
brosse à habits et une brosse à chapeaux
soies grises, montage
main (modèle déposé). **14.75**
Même composition, olivier verni. **23.** »

73 P 178 BROSSE à tête, soies pures
grises, extra-forte, montage main, bois
merisier verni. 9 rangs. 7 50 11 rangs. 8.90
Soies blanches 9 rangs.10.50 11 rangs. 12.90
Olivier verni 9 rangs. 13 50 11 rangs. 15. »

73- P -179. BROSSE
à ongles **5.50**
7 pans
Rectangulaire **5.25**

73-P-180
BROSSE à tête, brin
baleine spéciale pour
coiffure de dame, bois
façon citron
7 rangs **5.50**
8 rangs **5.90**
Brin corne blanche, façon
citron. 8 rangs. **6.90**
Brin corne blanche, ébène
forme boule 8 rangs. **11.90**

73-P-181
BROSSE à habits
soies pures grises, bo s
merisier verni, montage
main 8 rangs **9.90**
10 rangs **15.90**
En olivier verni
8 r 11.50 10 r 17.50
En palissandre, soies
pures, forme débord
9 rangs. 11.50 8 rangs. 9.90
En brin b
leine
6 rangs **6 25**
7 rangs **8 75**

89-P-709.
TONDEUSE sp
ale pour dame et
enfant
22. »

89 P-710.
FER à onduler, manche
couleur
5.90
Pour guiches, tout fer
2.10
Réchaud à friser
13. »

89-P-711.
DÉMÊLOIR deux den
tures en corne Irlande **3.25**
En écaille véritable jaspée **24.** »
Petit coiffeur pour homme,
écaille jaspée **18.** »

89-P-712.
PEIGNES-GUICHES
imperdables, décorés or. **7.90**
Les mêmes, unis **2.95**

73-P-191 BROSSE à ongles
bric-à-brac avec arête soies
pures bois buis
verni **11.50**

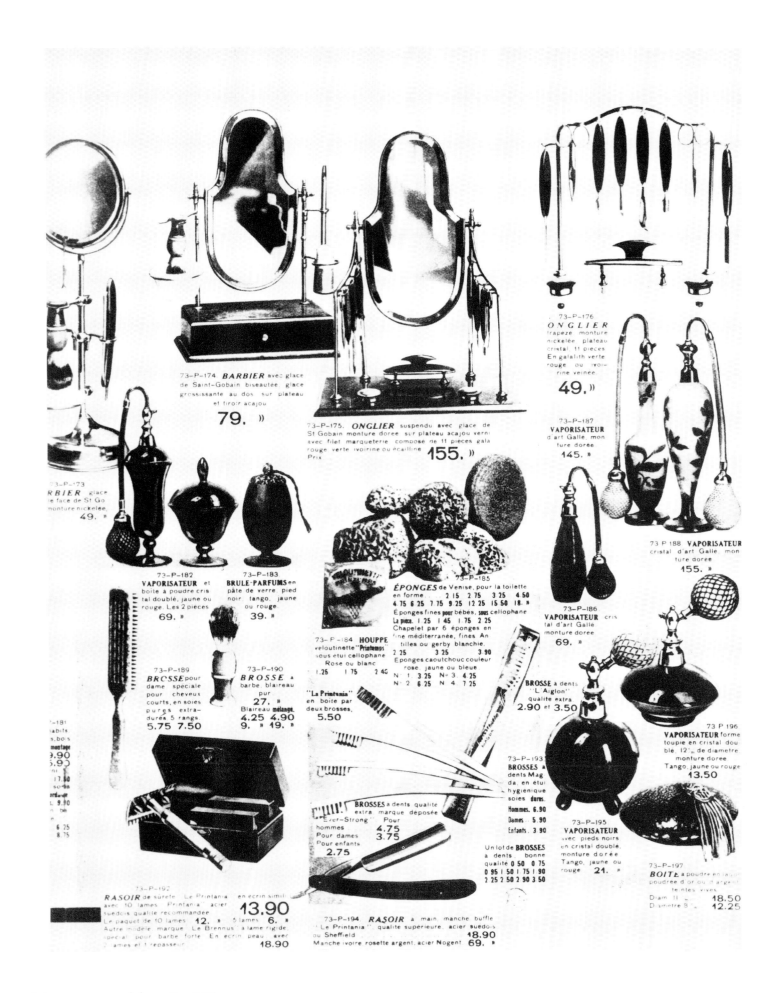

73-P-174 *BARBIER* avec glace de Saint-Gobain biseautée glace grossissante au dos sur plateau et tiroir acajou

79. »

73-P-175. *ONGLIER* suspendu avec glace de St Gobain monture dorée sur plateau acajou verni avec filet marqueterie composé de 11 pièces gala rouge verte ivoirine ou écaille
Prix **155.** »

73-P-176
ONGLIER trapèze monture nickelée plateau cristal 11 pièces En galalith verte rouge ou ivoirine veinée.
49. »

73-P-187
VAPORISATEUR d'art Gallé, monture dorée
145. »

73-P-173
BARBIER glace face de St Go monture nickelée.
49. »

73 P 188 *VAPORISATEUR* cristal d'art Gallé, monture dorée
155. »

73-P-182
VAPORISATEUR et boite à poudre cristal doublé, jaune ou rouge. Les 2 pièces
69. »

73-P-183
BRULE-PARFUMS en pâte de verre. pied noir tango. jaune ou rouge.
39. »

ÉPONGES de Venise, pour la toilette
en forme . 2 15 2 75   3 25   4 50
4 75 6 25 7 75 9 25 12 25 15 50 18. »
Éponges fines pour bébés, sous celophane
La pièce. 1 25   1 45   1 75   2 25
Chapelet par 6 éponges en fine méditerranée, fines An tilles ou gerby blanchie.
2 25   3 25   3 90
Éponges caoutchouc couleur rose, jaune ou bleue
N° 1. 3 25   N° 3. 4 25
N° 2. 6 25   N° 4. 7 25

73-P-185

73-P-186
VAPORISATEUR cristal d'art Gallé monture dorée
69. »

73-P-184 *HOUPPE* veloutinette "Printemps" sous étui celophane
Rose ou blanc
1 25   1 75   2 40

BROSSE pour dame spéciale pour cheveux courts, en soies pures extra dures 5 rangs.
73-P-189
5.75 7.50

73-P-190
BROSSE à barbe, blaireau pur
27. »
Blaireau mélangé.
4.25 4.90
9. » 19. »

"La Printania" en boite par deux brosses.
5.50

BROSSE à dents "L'Aiglon" qualité extra
2.90 et **3.50**

73 P 196
VAPORISATEUR forme toupie en cristal doublé. 12° de diamètre monture dorée Tango, jaune ou rouge
13.50

73-P-193
BROSSES à dents Magda, en étui hygiénique soies dures.
Hommes. 6.90
Dames. 5.90
Enfants. 3 90

BROSSES à dents qualité extra marque déposée "Ever-Strong" Pour hommes   4.75
Pour dames   3.75
Pour enfants
2.75

Un lot de BROSSES à dents. bonne qualité 0 50 0 75
0 95 1 50 1 75 1 90
2 25 2 50 2 90 3 50

73-P-195
VAPORISATEUR avec pieds noirs en cristal doublé. monture dorée Tango. jaune ou rouge **21.** »

73-P-197
BOITE à poudre en laque poudrée d'or ou d'argent teintes vives.
Diam 11 —   **18.50**
Diamètre 8 —   **12.25**

73-P-192
RASOIR de sûreté "Le Printania" en écrin simili avec 10 lames "Printania" acier suédois qualité recommandée
13.90
Le paquet de 10 lames **12.** » 5 lames **6.** »
Autre modèle marqué "Le Brennus" à lame rigide spécial pour barbe forte. En écrin peau avec 2 lames et 1 repasseur.
18.90

73-P-194 *RASOIR* à main, manche buffle "Le Printania", qualité supérieure, acier suédois ou Sheffield **18.90**
Manche ivoire rosette argent, acier Nogent **69.** »

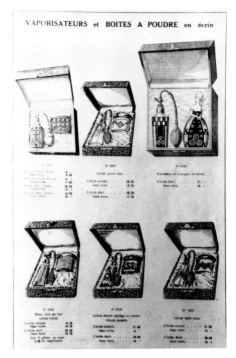

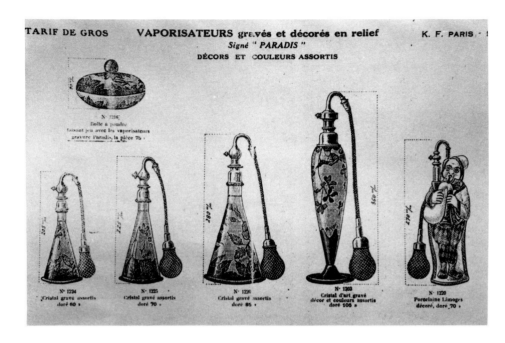

Kitzinger Frères catalogue, c.1922,
figuring atomizer/powder box gift
sets. Collection: Belle de Jour,
Montmartre, Paris.

1927 Kitzinger Frères catalogue
picturing a tardy line of cameo glass
atomizers in the Art Nouveau style
signed "Paradis", a tradename also
associated with Kitzinger Frères
pocket atomizers. Private collection.

1929 Galeries Lafayette catalogue.
Collection and photo: Bibliothèque
Forney, Ville de Paris.

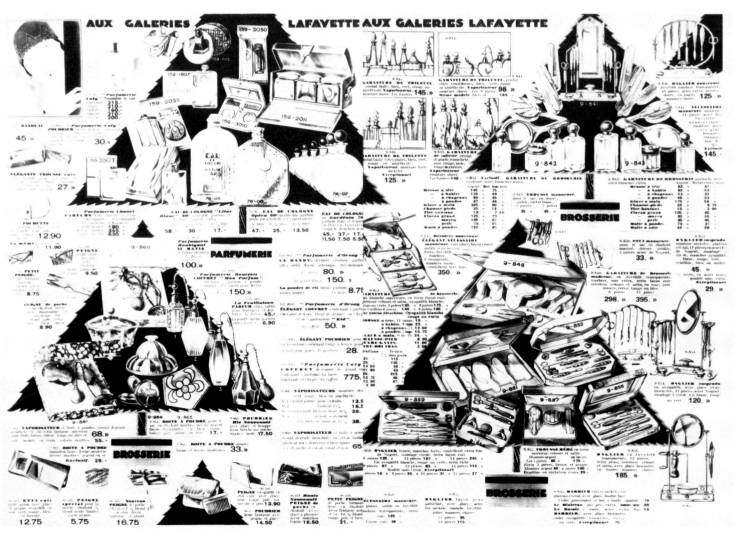

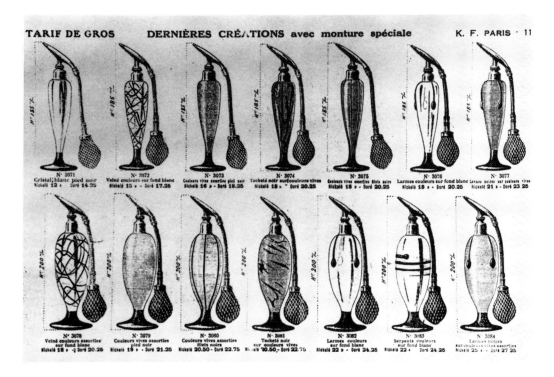

1927 Kitzinger Frères catalogue
featuring an array of stylish, double
crystal and enamelled glass models
with their sleek, 1920's mounts.
Private collection.

Catalogues from the Thirties

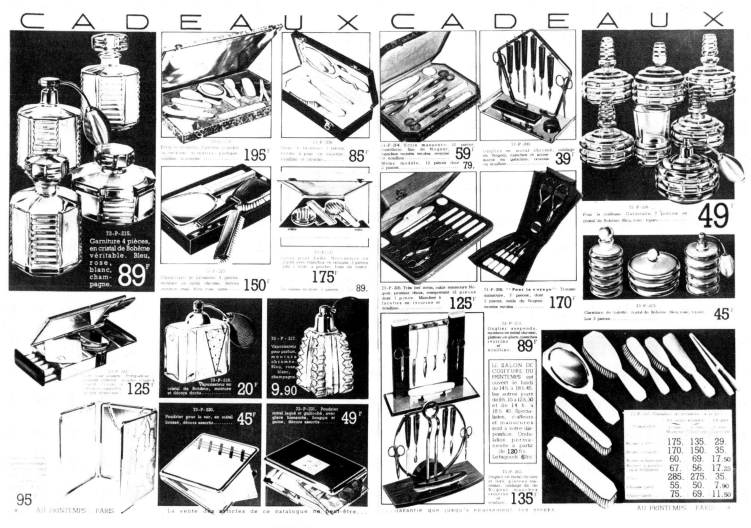

1937 Printemps catalogue. Collection
and photo: Bibliothèque Forney,
Ville de Paris.

1931 Galeries Lafayette catalogue.
Collection and photo: Bibliothèque
Forney, Ville de Paris.

Bibliography

Anscombe, Isabelle. *A Woman's Touch: Women in Design from 1860 to the Present Day*. NY: Elisabeth Sifton Books/Viking, 1984

Arwas, Victor. *Art Deco*. NY: Harry N Abrams, Inc., 1980

———. *Glass: Art Nouveau to Art Deco*. NY: Rizzoli, 1977

Battersby, Martin. *The Decorative Thirties*. NY: Walker and Co, 1971

———. *The Decorative Twenties*. London: Studio Vista/ Cassell & Collier MacMillan Publishers, Ltd., 1969

Bloch-Dermant, Janine. *L'Art du Verre en France 1860-1914*. Lausanne: Edita—DeNoel, 1974

———. *Le Verre en France d'Emile Gallé à nos Jours*. Paris: Les Editions de l'Amateur, 1983

Bowman, Leslie Greene. *American Arts & Crafts, Virtue in Design, a Catalogue of the Palevsky/Evans Collection & Related Works at the Los Angeles County Museum of Art*. Boston: Bulfinch Press/Little, Brown and Co., 1990

Brunhammer, Yvonne. *Art Deco Style*. London: Academy Editions, 1983

Brunhammer, Yvonne and Tise, Suzanne. *The Decorative Arts in France: La Société des Artistes Décorateurs 1900-1942*. NY: Rizzoli, 1990

Buffet-Challie, Laurence. *Art Nouveau Style*. NY: Rizzoli, 1982

Cooley, Arnold J.. *The Toilet and Cosmetic Arts in Ancient and Modern Times*, 1866

Delboug-Delphis, Marylène. *Sillage des Elégantes, Un Siècle d'Histoire des Parfums*. Paris: J.C. Latt, 1983

Duncan, Alastair. *American Art Deco*. NY: Harry N. Abrams, Inc., 1986

Launert, Edmund. *Perfume and Pomanders, Scent and Scent Bottles Through the Ages*. Potterton Books, Ltd., 1987

Louvre des Antiquaires. *Autour du Parfum du XVIe au XIXe Siecle*. Exhibition Catalogue, Paris, 1985

———. *Charles Schneider, Maitre Verrier, Verreries Schneider France de 1913 à 1940*. Exhibition Catalogue, Paris, 1984

Marchilac, Félix. *Lalique, Catalogue Raisonné de l'oeuvre de René Lalique*, Paris, 1989

———. *René Lalique, Maitre-Verrier*. Paris: Editions de l'Amateur, 1989

Musée d'Art et d'Histoire, Grasse. *3000 Ans de Parfumerie, Parfums, Savons, Fards, et Cosmétiques, de l'Antiquité à nos Jours*. Exhibition Catalogue, Grasse, 1980

Musée des Arts Décoratifs. *Cinquantenaire de l' Exposition de 1925*. Exhibition Catalogue, Paris, 1976-77

Musée des Beaux Arts de Nancy. *Daum, Cent Ans de Verre et de Cristal*. Exhibition Catalogue, Nancy, 1977

———. *Daum, Cent Ans de Création dans le Verre et le Cristal*. Exhibition Catalogue, Nancy, 1978-79

Musée du Luxembourg. *Gallé*. Exhibition Catalogue, Paris, 1985-86

Musée de la Mode et du Costume, Palais Galliera. *Paul Poiret et Nicole Groult, Maitres de la Mode Art Déco.* Exhibition Catalogue, Paris, 1986

Nathan, Fernand. *La Belle Epoque, 1900-1914, Les Illusions Délicieuses de l' Europe pendant Quinze Ans de son Existence.* Milano: Arnoldo Mondador, Editore, 1977

Nicolle, Rose. *Une Idée de Parisienne par Page.* Paris: Editions Nilsson, c.1910

North, Jacqueline Y. Jones. *Commercial Perfume Bottle.* West Chester: Schiffer Publishing, Ltd., 1987

_____ . *Perfume, Cologne, and Scent Bottles.* West Chester: Schiffer Publishing, Ltd., 1986

Piesse, Septimus. *Des Odeurs et des Parfums.* Baillère: 1877

_____ . *Histoire des Parfums.* 1905

Revue des Marques, La Parfumerie Française et l'Art dans la Présentation, 1925.

Sloan, Jean. *Perfume and Scent Bottle Collecting.* Lombard: Wallace Homestead Book Co., 1986

Steele, Valerie. *Paris Fashion: A Cultural History.* Oxford: Oxford University Press, 1988

Tramar, La Comtesse de. *Le Brèviaire de la Femme.* Paris: 1906

Union Centrale des Arts Décoratifs. *Le Livre des Expositions Universelles, 1851-1989.* Exhibition Catalogue, Paris, 1983

Vigarello, Georges. *Le Propre et le Sale, l' Hygiène du Corps depuis le Moyen Age.* Paris: Seuil, 1985

INDEX

VALUE GUIDE

Values vary immensely according to the piece's condition, location of the market, and overall quality of design. While one must make their own decisions, we can offer a guide. All values listed are U.S. dollars ($). Copyright © 1991 by Schiffer Publishing Ltd., 1469 Morstein Road, West Chester, PA 19380

Key: T=Top, C=Center, B=Bottom, R=Right, L=Left, N/A= Price Not Available

Page #	Value
2	200
6	150
7	75
9	150
10	100
11, L	250
11, R	200
12	each, +/-150
13	400
15, R	175
16, R	100
17	each, +/-130
18, TL	each, 75
18, R	60
18, B	75
20	each, +/-25
21	125
22, L	40
22, R	60
23, TL	130
23, R	200
24, TL	60
24, R & BL	N/A
26, L & R	N/A
27, T & B	N/A
28, TL & R	N/A
28, B	set, 225
32	80
33, L	atomizer only, 60
33, TR	80
33, BR	75
34, L	75
34, R	85
35, T & B	N/A
36, TL	N/A
36, TR	75
38	1,500
40	1,000
41	2,000
42	80
43	N/A
44	N/A
45	60
46	75
47, L	80
47, TR	each, 50
47, BR	25
48, L	75
48, TR	30

Page #	Value
48, BR	each, +/-75
49, TL	40
49, TR	100
49, B	each, +/-80
50, L	45
50, TR	25
50, BR	100
51	125
52, L	60
52, R	225
53, TL	50
53, R	100
53, BL	35
54, TL	40
54, C	35
54, BR	40
55, L	75
55, TR	150
55, BR	N/A
56	750
57, L & R	N/A
58, T	850
58, BL & BR	N/A
59, TR	800
60	1,300
61	1,100
62	800
63, TR	125
63, BL	N/A
64, TL	N/A
65, TR & BR	N/A
65, BL	75
66	350
67, TL	400
67, BR	N/A
68, TL	N/A
69, TL	N/A
69, TR	50
69, BL	100
69, BR	each, +/-40
70, T	N/A
70, B	75
71	N/A
73	450
74, TL	100
74, BL	500
75, TL	50
75, C	100
75, BL	100
75, BR	125
76, T	80
76, B	set, 500
77, T	set, 500
77, BL	75
77, BR	75
78, L	100
78, BR	80
79, T	75
79, B	each, +/-60
80, T	set, 130
80, B	80
81, L	100
81, R	100
82, L	80
82, R	N/A
83, T	set, 110
83, B	80
84, L	70
84, R	75
85, L	100
85, TR	100
85, C & BR	N/A
86, TL & TR	N/A
86, BL	25
86, BR	135

Page #	Value
87, TL	60
87, C	80
87, BR	80
88, TL	60
88, C	75
88, BR	50
92, L	150
92, TR	80
92, BR	80
93, L	250
93, R	80
94, TL	80
94, TR	(damaged) 50
94, BL	80
94, BR	atomizer 150
95, L	175
95, R	each, +/-70
96, T	100
96, BL	70
96, BR	each, +/-70
97, T	100
97, B	70
98, TL	35
98, TR	150
98, B	150
99	80
100, L	80
100, TR	set, 120
100, BR	set, 150
101	350
102, TL	60
102, C	100
102, BL	25
103, L	300
103, TR	25
103, BR	100
104, L	100
104, R	125
105, TL	75
105, TR	100
105, B	65
106, L	N/A
106, R	90
108, T	75
108, B	85
109, TL	80
109, TR	60
110, T	110
110, BL	70
110, BR	80
111, T	60
111, B	each, +/-200
112	with case, 300
113, L	200
113, TR	185
113, BR	180
114, T	70
114, C	80
114, B	50
115, TL	30
115, R	70
115, BL	30
116, TL	30
116, TR	70
116, B	70
117, TL	70
117, TR	N/A
117, BL	40
117, BC	15
117, BR	40
120, B	200
125	set, 120
126	200
128, TL	85
128, BL	N/A

Page #	Value
128, BR	85
129, TL	20
129, TR	70
129, BL	20
130, T	N/A
130, B	each, +/-90
131, T	atomizer only, 40
131, B	35
132, TL	with case,125
132, TR	40
132, BL	40
133	130
135	N/A
137	40
138	65
139, T	65
139, B	N/A
140, T	125
140, B	80
141, CR	80
142, TL	N/A
142, TR	80
142, BL	N/A
142, BR	N/A
143, L & R	N/A